WISE UP

TERRY POWELL

VICTOR BOOKS®

A DIVISION OF SCRIPTURE PRESS PUBLICATIONS INC.
USA CANADA ENGLAND

Wise Up is a study on the Book of Proverbs for high school students. It explores the "nuggets" of God's advice found in the book and demonstrates how we can apply that advice to our lives today. Student activity booklets (Rip-Off Sheets) and a leader's guide with visual aids (SonPower Multiuse Transparency Masters) are available from your local Christian bookstore or from the publisher.

Unless otherwise indicated, Scripture is taken from the *Holy Bible, New International Version,* © 1973, 1978, 1984, International Bible Society. Used by permission of Zondervan Bible Publishers. Other Scripture quotations are from the *New American Standard Bible* (NASB), © the Lockman Foundation 1960, 1962, 1963, 1968, 1971, 1972, 1973, 1975, 1977. Scripture quotations marked PH are from J.B. Phillips: *The New Testament in Modern English,* Revised Edition, © J.B. Phillips, 1958, 1960, 1972, permission of Macmillan Publishing Co. and Collins Publishers. Other Scripture quotations are from the *Authorized (King James) Version* (KJV).

Library of Congress Catalog Card Number: 90-81688

ISBN: 0-89693-818-2

Recommended Dewey Decimal Classification: 248.83
Suggested Subject Heading: YOUTH — RELIGIOUS LIFE

1 2 3 4 5 6 7 8 9 10 Printing/Year 94 93 92 91 90

CONTENTS

This book is
affectionately dedicated to

Stephen Floyd Powell,

the Boy Wonder of weightlifting.
His name means "victor's crown."
May the wisdom of God's Word make
him a winner in the contests that
count for eternity.

1

PERSPECTIVE
FROM PROVERBS

Picture yourself as a college freshman. You have two problems common among students: low grades and no money. You need to break the news of both to your parents, but you figure they'll have trouble understanding. What strategy would you use?

In his book, *Growing Strong in the Seasons of Life* (Multnomah), Charles Swindoll tells about a coed in precisely this situation. She used a creative approach to soften the blows of reality. The following is an excerpt of the letter she wrote to break the news to her parents:

Dear Mom and Dad,
    Just thought I'd drop you a note to clue you

in on my plans. I've fallen in love with a guy named Jim. He quit high school after grade eleven to get married. About a year ago he got a divorce.

We've been going steady for two months and plan to get married in the fall. Until then, I've decided to move into his apartment (I think I might be pregnant).

At any rate, I dropped out of school last week, although I'd like to finish college sometime in the future.

On the next page she continued:

Mom and Dad, I just want you to know that everything I've written so far in this letter is false. NONE of it is true.

But Mom and Dad, it IS true that I got a C in French and flunked Math. It IS true that I'm going to need some more money for my tuition payments.

Commenting on the letter, Swindoll writes:

Pretty sharp coed! Even bad news can sound like good news if it is seen from a certain vantage point. So much in life depends on "where you're coming from" as you face your circumstances. The secret, of course, is perspective.

The View from Mount Perspective

Perspective. Just as the coed used it to her advantage, so can you. According to *Webster's New Collegiate Dictionary,* perspective is "the capacity to view things in their true relations or relative importance." Put simply, it's the ability to see issues clearly, to distinguish the temporary from the eternal, the important from the trivial. The coed knew that poor grades and an empty pocketbook were minor matters compared to the fictional circumstances in her letter.

Whether or not we cultivate an accurate perspective on life depends on who shapes our attitudes and values. So, let me put the question to you—Who shapes your attitudes and values? Who prescribes the lenses you look through when you view other people and things that go on around you? What's the source of the assumptions and convictions that forge your behavior from day to day?

If you are a Christian, then it should be God who prescribes your lenses. How we view things—and ultimately, how we act—should match up with *His* perceptions. The lens which gives us God's viewpoint is the Bible. And if Christians fail to see life experiences through the perspective lens of Scripture, we'll find ourselves following the dinosaurs to extinction.

That's why I wrote this paperback on the Book of Proverbs: to examine God's perspectives on everyday things like the relationships you establish and the choices you make. Who doesn't need to tap into God's wisdom and see issues from His vantage point?

In *You and Your Network,* Fred Smith said, "No one is eager to learn anything he isn't going to use shortly." Bank on it: the material we will explore in Proverbs will be usable the day you read it! Studying this ancient book is like getting a Ph.D. in living. Its content is as up-to-date as the latest issue of *People* magazine. I'm not trying to dump obsolete material on you. The following questions provide a sampling of the subjects discussed in Proverbs:

● What are the consequences of self-indulgence?

● How can I avoid moral erosion in an X-rated culture?

- What effect do my friends have on my character?
- How should I respond when I'm criticized?
- When I'm pressed to make decisions about my future, what guidelines can help me?
- What does the Bible mean when it says to "fear the Lord"? Am I supposed to cringe in His presence?
- Why is pride considered "Public Enemy #1" for the Christian?
- What's the best way to use and invest my money?
- What is a "godly" woman?
- In what specific ways can my tongue get me in trouble? How can I control it?
- What are some tips for confronting people when I need to?

A Christian chemistry professor at a large university told his students, "Christianity is not a lecture. It is a laboratory science."

Bull's-eye! We confirm our faith in Christ not by passing a theology quiz, but through daily experimentation. And the laboratory can be your school cafeteria or the den of your home, not just the church sanctuary or Sunday School classroom. Studying the topics in Proverbs will help you *exercise* your faith, not just cram more biblical data into the recesses of your mind.

Before we delve into these topics, let me formally introduce you to the Old Testament Book of Proverbs.

Transistorized Wisdom
To help familiarize you with the nature of Proverbs, I turn to a parable Calvin Miller tells in *The Taste of Joy* (InterVarsity). The story concerns a king who ordered his wise men to condense all human wisdom into as few words as possible:

They [the wise men] returned after twelve years of work with twelve thick volumes. "It is too large," protested the king. "Condense it further!" So the wise men returned in a year and presented one large volume in place of the twelve. "It's still too large," protested the king. They went out again, only to return the following day with a single statement written on a slip of paper—all the world's wisdom in one line: *There is no free lunch.*

In Proverbs, you can get the scoop on God's perspective without having to plow through a textbook in theology. Like a transistor radio that fits in your shirt pocket, the sayings in Proverbs are spiritual transistors that can readily be stored in your heart.

Most Bible books you read come in the form of a narrative, which tells a story, or a letter filled with advice from a leader to a group of believers. Not Proverbs. It's a thirty-one-chapter catalog of short, pithy remarks on everything from keeping a lid on your temper to the side effects of too much booze. Unlike most Bible books, a verse you read in Proverbs may cover an entirely different topic than the verse before or after it.

Our English term for "proverb" comes from two Latin words which mean "instead of words." So a *proverb* is a sentence of condensed wisdom that's offered in place of a whole spate of words. The writers "get to the point" by summarizing a general principle of life with a particular illustration. For instance, ponder Proverbs 11:22: "Like a gold ring in a pig's snout is a beautiful woman who shows no discretion." An entire book could not drive home the point any better: *Poor character spoils a woman's physical attractiveness.*

Scholars credit King Solomon with the proverbs in chapters 1–24 of the collection. Around 950 years before Christ, he either wrote or compiled these bits of advice. What you find in chapters 25–31 is divinely sanctioned wisdom from other sources.

Poetic Justice

The long-range goal of the paperback you're holding is to give you a taste of the smorgasbord of truth in Proverbs, so you'll make this taken-for-granted part of Scripture a staple item in your spiritual diet. Long after *Wise Up* is out of print, Proverbs will offer fresh menus for you to choose from. But before you start sampling the morsels God dishes up in this book of the Bible, it's important to understand the type of literature it represents. Otherwise, it's easy to get the wrong meaning out of a verse. To get its messages across, Proverbs employs *poetic* language, including numerous figures of speech. In his book, *The House on the Rock* (Victor), Charles Sell describes the nature of a proverb:

> When a colleague of mine and I were teaching a class together, he created a proverb of his own to explain their nature . . . . "Walk in the mud and your shoes will get muddy." . . . When my fellow teacher spoke of mud, everyone knew he wasn't giving a lesson about clean shoes. He was warning us to stay away from pornography, drugs, bad company, and other negative influences. That's the genius of a proverb: it makes an obvious statement to get across a not-so-obvious truth.

We can't interpret comments in Proverbs in the same way we interpret statements of fact, such as

"It's snowing outside." Instead, we must find the general message or broad principle in a proverb without turning it into a rigidly absolute statement. Again let's learn from Charles Sell regarding this sticky issue of interpretation.

> The Hebrews tended to make general statements without worrying about the exceptions, appealing to the reader's common sense to see this. For example, Proverbs 16:3 assures success to those who first commit their plans to God. But committing alone does not guarantee prosperity; many persons trust God to help them fulfill foolish goals. The proverb is not true for them.
>
> Because they are principles, we must also not turn all of them into promises from God. God is using the wise writers of the proverbs to describe what *usually* occurs in life. For example, one proverb states, "When a man's ways are pleasing to the Lord, He makes even his enemies live at peace with him" (16:7). The principle here is that being rightly related to God will keep you rightly related to others. God doesn't guarantee this will always happen. Jesus was without sin, yet He was murdered by His enemies. *(The House on the Rock)*

Neither can we take the figures of speech found in Proverbs literally. When you come across Proverbs 6:29, you'll read that a man who *touches* another man's wife will be punished. Does that mean you'll go to jail for accidently bumping into a lady in the ticket line of the theater? No. The word *touch* is obviously a polite way of talking about having sex with her. Or consider the way Proverbs 15:25 exaggerates in order to get a point across: "The Lord tears down the proud man's house but He keeps the widow's boundaries intact." This type of statement is called a hyperbole, a figure of speech which overstates a matter in order to convey a message. The author wasn't promising that the minute pride infects your dad, the walls of your room will collapse. But he was saying that God resists the proud and defends the helpless.

I could drone on about the different literary forms in Proverbs. But I don't want your eyelids to get stuck at half-mast during this opening chapter.

Precious Cargo

In 1985, deep-sea divers located the treasure of the sunken Spanish galleon *Nuestra Senora de Atocha.* The leader of the expedition, Mel Fisher, and his crew hauled to the surface $400 million worth of gold and silver bars, and emeralds by the quart. Experts estimated the total value of the salvage at $4 billion!

We envy this fortune hunter until we discover the price he paid for the search. Mel Fisher had been crisscrossing the ocean for fifteen frustrating years looking for that sunken ship, at a cost of $70 million. Some of his crew members went without pay for six years. And here's a more sobering fact: The treasure hunt cost Mel Fisher the lives of his son and daughter-in-law, who had drowned when their hunting vessel capsized in a storm (Francis Norris, "$400 Million Treasure: A Record Find Off Key West," *Motor Boating and Sailing,* October 1985; and "Spanish Wreck Bursting With Emeralds," *Chicago Tribune,* 29 May 1986).

Are we that committed to salvaging the precious cargo of Proverbs? You can forget right now any idea that God drops His gems of insight into our laps without any work on our part. We won't pay as steep a price as Mel Fisher, yet claiming the fortune in Proverbs will cost us some time and effort. If you honestly want God's perspective on the things that matter most to you, read the next ten chapters in this paperback. Then make treasure-hunting through Proverbs a lifetime hobby. "If you look for it [wisdom] as for silver and search for it as for hidden treasure, then you will understand the fear of the Lord and find the knowledge of God" (Proverbs 2:4-5).

Here's a reading schedule to guide you in your journey through Proverbs. Digest a chapter a day, corresponding to the day of the month. If it's August 5, read Proverbs 5, and so on. When you miss a day, don't fret over making up the previous chapter. You can make it up the following month, when you read through the Book of Proverbs again. Such repeated exposure is the only way God's wisdom can nuzzle its way into your mind and heart.

2

THE FOOLISH
WISE MAN

When you see or hear the name Einstein, what pops into your mind? If you're like most people, you equate the name with a mathematics marvel who lived a few decades ago. Perhaps you've called the smartest person in your class an "Einstein." (You know him: the guy who aces every quiz, who visits the public library on Friday nights, and who thinks summer school is fun.)

The original Albert Einstein was so brainy that it's even difficult to understand his accomplishments. He taught us a lot about the universe by developing the "theory of relativity." He proved the Pythagorean theorem: The square of the length of the hypotenuse of a right triangle is equal to the sum of the squares of the lengths of the other two sides. Einstein also mastered the theory of electromagnetism. (See what I mean? It takes an "Einstein" just to figure out what he did!)

You would probably assume that Einstein was a teacher's pet. You figure that teachers would have loved to put him into a Xerox machine, push the button, and place a copy of Albert behind every desk. Good grades were a cinch for him, right?

Wrong! Einstein was a scientific genius, all right. But he didn't exactly fit the mold of the "most-likely-to-succeed" student. Mull over the following facts:

As a child, he gave no hint of becoming a genius. Most children begin talking before their second birthday. Little Albert didn't talk until after his third birthday!

Einstein's teachers didn't like him. A Greek teacher once told him, "You will never amount to anything!" In the seventh grade, his homeroom teacher asked him to leave school. When Albert told him that he had done nothing wrong, the teacher replied, "Your mere presence spoils the respect of the class for me." Several times he switched schools because he couldn't get along with his teachers.

A poor memory handicapped his learning. While an old man, Einstein wrote, "As a pupil I was neither particularly good nor bad. My principal weakness was a poor memory and especially a poor memory for words and texts."

Late in his career he taught at Princeton Graduate School in New Jersey. One day the secretary received a phone call from a man asking for Dr. Einstein's address. To protect Dr. Einstein's privacy, she refused to give the address to the caller. The voice on the telephone dropped to a whisper: "Please do not tell anybody, but *I* am Dr. Einstein. I am on my way home, and have forgotten where my house is!"

As a 16-year-old, he failed the entrance exam for the Federal Institute of Technology in Switzerland. Poor scores in subjects like languages and botany frustrated him.

He couldn't keep his mind on teachers' lectures, so he rarely took any notes. (Does that sound familiar?) If a classmate hadn't loaned Albert his class notes, Einstein might have failed his college finals (Terry Powell, "The Genius Who Hated School," *Dash,* October/November 1976).

I don't know about you, but I was surprised to uncover those facts about the century's most towering mental giant. Because his I.Q. was higher than the Himalayas, we tend to think school was a breeze for him. Who'd guess that a man of Einstein's caliber would make his share of poor grades, and drive teachers into early retirement?

Similarly, what we learn about some characters from the Bible can surprise us too. The images stamped on our minds back in Vacation Bible School don't always reveal the whole story.

Solomon is a case in point. His name is synonymous with wisdom. Some of us have heard accolades about his distinguished discernment since we were knee-high to a gnat. So we figure that if anybody had a handle on life, it was Solomon. If there was anyone in Palestine who didn't need to consult "Dear Abby," it was Solomon, the Jewish king whose sound counsel to others raised eyebrows from border to border. His cunning got him out of more scrapes than Indiana Jones, right?

Wrong. The fact is, a series of clumsy choices imprisoned Solomon in his own "Temple of Doom." When it came to the tests posed by life situations, Solomon couldn't make the grade. The older he got, the more foolishly he acted. The proverbs he wrote are right on target. But he didn't practice what he preached.

This chapter explains the irony of his life, and tells why he was the most foolish wise man who ever lived. Reading the story of Solomon can improve *your* grade point average in the school of daily experience. Soak up the lessons from his life, and watch your spiritual I.Q. zoom to Einstein proportions.

Star-studded Success

When Solomon was just 15 years old, he inherited the throne of Israel. A quick glance at his forty-year reign shows a public relations dream come true. Solomon's reign launched an era of peace and prosperity for Israel. His early popularity eclipsed even that of his father, King David.

Solomon's list of achievements reads like a page out of *Who's Who*. He wrote at least 3,000 proverbs and 1,005 songs. He had a college-level knowledge of botany, zoology, horticulture, architecture, philosophy, and literature. As a result of his diplomacy, Israel's borders expanded to their greatest geographical extent. Residents of nearby nations shook in their sandals at the size of his military stockpile. To top it all off, he was wealthier than any Wall Street financial wizard. His personal residence was so lavish that it would make a Beverly Hills mansion look like an inner-city ghetto project.

What accounted for Solomon's political savvy and bulging bank account? "The Lord his God was with him and made him exceedingly great" (2 Chronicles

1:1). God was Solomon's Secretary of State, chief of staff, PR expert, and investment broker all rolled into one. God prospered him because, as an adolescent ruler, Solomon revealed a unique spiritual sensitivity.

His inauguration was still front-page news when he begged God for the wisdom needed to fulfill his job description: "Give Your servant a discerning heart to govern Your people and to distinguish between right and wrong. For who is able to govern this great people of Yours?" (1 Kings 3:9). Solomon's humility impressed God so much that, in addition to giving Solomon the *wisdom* he asked for, God also threw in material prosperity as a bonus. "I will do what you have asked. I will give you a wise and discerning heart, so that there will never have been anyone like you, nor will there ever be. Moreover, I will give you what you have not asked for – both riches and honor" (1 Kings 3:12-13). It's clear that as a young man, Solomon followed his own advice about relying on God: "Trust in the Lord with all your heart, and lean not on your own understanding" (Proverbs 3:5).

Because the Lord pushed all the buttons, "Solomon's wisdom was greater than the wisdom of all the men of the East, and greater than all the wisdom of Egypt. . . . And his fame spread to all the surrounding nations" (1 Kings 4:30-31).

Before you start drooling over Solomon's advantages though, remember this: he ran out of gas before reaching the finish line. He became intoxicated by too many gulps of worldly pleasure. He started living life according to his own script, instead of God's. Lets discover how disobedience diluted his character.

Crafty Compromise

Here's how the dictionary defines *compromise:* "to make a shameful or disreputable concession." It's making a choice based on personal rewards at the expense of ethical convictions. To use contemporary examples, compromise is copying someone else's paper despite a deep-rooted conviction against cheating, or taking illegal steroids to gain an unfair advantage on the athletic field.

Compromise with God's Word revealed termites in the timber of Solomon's character. One minute he'd pray zealously to the Lord. The next minute he'd make a decision that left God with the short end of the stick. For an example of his inconsistent allegiance, turn to 1 Kings 3:1. He took a step of political expediency when he "made an alliance with Pharaoh king of Egypt and married his daughter" and "brought her to the City of David." The royal wedding served as a peace treaty with Egypt. Yet Solomon knew God had forbidden Jews to marry people from foreign countries. He would later discover that the price he paid for peace with the Egyptians was inflationary.

Another example of Solomon's sacrificing conviction at the altar of convenience is found in 1 Kings 3:3: "Solomon showed his love for the Lord by walking according to the statutes of his father David, *except he offered sacrifices and burned incense on the high places*" (emphasis mine). The "high places" referred to altars erected for the worship of idols. To pacify people around him who clung to the false gods of the Canaanites, Solomon protected their worship centers. He knew their gods didn't exist, yet he even participated in the pagan worship services just to keep the people on his side. His refusal to wipe out the pagan altars defied a previous command handed down by Moses: "Break down their altars, smash their sacred stones" (Deuteronomy 7:5).

Imagine that Billy Graham joined Muslims in a pilgrimage to Mecca and in a prayer to Allah just to improve his image in the Middle East (of course, Dr. Graham wouldn't make such a compromise)—that's the kind of fence-straddling faith Solomon had. He feared the opinion of men more than the consequences of sin. He failed to heed the advice he had given others about righteousness: "The integrity of the upright guides them, but the unfaithful are destroyed by their duplicity" (Proverbs 11:3).

First Kings 11:6 says that the seed of compromise sprouted from the shallow soil of Solomon's half-hearted commitment to God: he "did not follow the Lord completely." Almost 3,000 years have passed, yet such fickle fidelity toward the Lord is still as common as a sore throat in January. Like Solomon, too many of us try to serve the Lord without offending the devil.

Anthony Munoz didn't mind offending Satan, though. Munoz is a perennial All-Pro offensive lineman for the Cincinnati Bengals. He played in the 1989 Super Bowl. Prior to the start of the 1986 season, *Playboy* magazine wanted to interview Munoz for a major sports story about key "matchups" between offensive and defensive players in the NFL. Enter the temptation for this Christian athlete to compromise. "This was a story about the best guys in the league, which made it an honor of sorts to be singled out," explained Munoz. "*Playboy* wanted to fly me out for a day of interviews and pics."

But the readers of *Playboy's* "Pigskin Preview" that summer didn't find Cincinnati's premier lineman splashed between the indecent photos of the opposite sex. After praying and consulting with his pastor, Munoz turned down the interview. He declined because the magazine isn't compatible with his moral beliefs. More important than pumping up his athletic image was exercising his convictions. "With my beliefs as a Christian, I couldn't see myself doing it," said Munoz ("Anthony Munoz Blocks *Playboy* at the Line of Scrimmage," *Focus On The Family*, May 1987).

Munoz understood what Thomas Carlyle meant when he wrote, "Conviction is worthless unless it is converted into conduct." Munoz also avoided the "domino effect" of a single act of compromise. Just as you can topple a whole row of dominoes with a slight shove on the first one, you can start a chain reaction of destructive choices with one instance of rationalization. One decision to shuck your values makes it that much easier the next time.

Solomon "loved the Lord, *except. . . .*" Is there an "except clause" in *your* devotion to God?

Enough Wasn't Enough
You already know that God granted Solomon's request for wisdom. And on top of that, the Lord made an eye-popping deposit in Solomon's bank account. He threw in riches as a bonus because Solomon had made an unselfish, humble request. So the king's possessions didn't pose a spiritual problem—until his possessions pulled a political coup and stole God's place on the throne of Solomon's heart. Before long, Solomon developed a thirst for *things* that couldn't be quenched.

Having a lot of things wasn't Solomon's problem. His problem was a craving for more. Greed caused dissatisfaction with God's gifts, and injected the poison of a "more" mentality into Solomon's bloodstream.

Before the first king was ever crowned in Israel, God had warned future rulers about the energy-sapping pull of greed. He had left explicit instructions for each king to read: "The king . . . must not acquire great numbers of horses for himself. . . . He must not accumulate large amounts of silver and gold" (Deuteronomy 17:16-17).

Perhaps God dropped wealth into Solomon's lap early in his reign so the king wouldn't have to worry about his next meal, or the threat of the palace electricity being turned off. Then, since Solomon had plenty, he could focus his attention on governing the people. Yet Solomon didn't cooperate with God's intentions. He spent as much time and energy managing his money as he did serving the country.

A tip-off to Solomon's love for luxury was the time it took to build his personal palace. The temple he built for God was finished in seven years. Construction of his own residence took thirteen years! His expensive tastes resulted in crippling taxation of his subjects. In a business transaction with King Hiram of Tyre, Solomon traded several cities in Galilee for building supplies. When it came time for Hiram to claim the cities, their skyline didn't impress him. He felt jilted in the trade-off. There's no record of Solomon ever trying to make things right. When greed reigns, our consciences go into rigor mortis. We start valuing things more than people. The irony is that Solomon himself warned people about putting things above relationships: "Better a little with the fear of the Lord than great wealth with turmoil. Better a meal of vegetables where there is love than a fatted calf with hatred" (Proverbs 15:16-17).

Notice how an uncontrolled appetite can lead to a tragic conclusion:

Radio personality Paul Harvey tells the story of how an Eskimo kills a wolf. The account is grisly, yet it offers fresh insight into the consuming, self-destructive nature of sin.

"First the Eskimo coats his knife blade with

animal blood and allows it to freeze. Then he adds another layer of blood, and another, until the blade is completely concealed by frozen blood.

Next, the hunter fixes his knife in the ground with the blade up. When a wolf follows his sensitive nose to the source of the scent and discovers the bait he licks it, tasting the fresh-frozen blood. He begins to lick faster, more and more vigorously, lapping the blade until the keen edge is bare. Feverishly now, harder and harder the wolf licks the blade in the Arctic night. So great becomes his craving for blood that the wolf does not notice the razor sharp sting of the naked blade on his tongue nor does he recognize the instant at which his insatiable thirst is being satisfied by his *own* warm blood. His carnivorous appetite just craves more — until the dawn finds him dead in the snow!" (Chris Zwingelberg, "Sin's Peril," *Leadership* #8, Winter 1987)

Unless we put a rein on our craving for things, it will consume our appetite for God. As an old man, looking back on his lavish lifestyle, the sharp blade of regret slashed Solomon's conscience. Writing in his journal, he first acknowledged his material bent: "I built houses for myself and planted vineyards . . . amassed silver and gold. . . . I denied myself nothing my eyes desired" (Ecclesiastes 2:4, 8, 10). Did all these lucrative investments satisfy his soul? Just the opposite. He concluded: "Everything was meaningless, a chasing after the wind; nothing was gained under the sun" (2:11). A hollow human heart bleeds more than a wolf carcass lying in the Arctic snow.

THE FOOLISH WISE MAN

Losing to Lust

Little by little Solomon's character decayed. To the erosive sins of compromise and materialism, add an addiction to sex. In the personal journal referred to earlier, he also confessed, "I acquired . . . a harem as well—the delights of the heart of man" (Ecclesiastes 2:8).

According to 1 Kings 11:3, Solomon had 700 wives and 300 concubines. When he wasn't huddling with his banker, he was hopping in bed with someone he hardly knew. The wives and concubines had to take a number just to get a date with him. Solomon slept around despite a divine directive for sexual purity. In the same breath in which Moses warned future kings about materialism, he said, "He must not take many wives, or his heart will be led astray" (Deuteronomy 17:17).

What was the effect of lust on Solomon? His harem drained him of affection for God. The wives from non-Jewish backgrounds diverted his attention away from Jehovah to their idols. They "turned his heart away after other gods" (1 Kings 11:4). Perhaps John was meditating on Solomon when he wrote, "If anyone loves the world, the love of the Father is not in him" (1 John 2:15). Solomon's X-rated lifestyle infected his heart, immunizing him to the truth of God's Word.

Solomon would nod in agreement with David Morley's observation: "The sex drive is so intense that it can cut across all lines of judgment and intelligence. It can make a man cheat, steal, or kill, or make him throw away all his wealth or talent in order to pursue it" (*HIS*, November 1971).

Sensuality was a mirage for Solomon. He thought it would satisfy a thirst for pleasure. Instead, the heat of his passion resulted in a barren, parched heart. Yet he knew better, for it was Solomon who wrote the following warning about sexual sin: "Can a man scoop fire into his lap without his clothes being burned? Can a man walk on hot coals without his feet being scorched?" (Proverbs 6:27-38)

Sowing and Reaping

Solomon's all-you-can-eat buffet lifestyle eventually led to heartburn. And it was the kind of pain he couldn't cure with a dose of Pepto-Bismol. His brazen defiance was an invitation for the Lord to discipline him. Scripture makes it clear that God didn't ignore the severity of Solomon's sins. Consequences came in the following forms:

● *God's anger.* For a long time God exercised patience with Solomon's inconsistency. But when Solomon dabbled in idolatry to pacify his foreign wives, that was the last straw! "The Lord became angry with Solomon because his heart had turned away from the Lord, the God of Israel. . . . Although he had forbidden Solomon to follow other gods, Solomon did not keep the Lord's command" (1 Kings 11:9-10).

The Bible makes it crystal clear that God is slow to anger, and forgiving. But His unconditional love shouldn't lull us into believing that He's soft and tolerant toward sin. His concern for us causes Him to discipline us. He will permit pain in our lives as an attention-getting device. One type of psychological pain experienced by Solomon was broken fellowship with his Creator.

● *Internal rebellion.* One of the judgments stemming from God's anger was a split kingdom. Solomon had worked long and hard for a united empire. One of his long-term goals was to eliminate internal factions as well as foreign enemies. Yet God's axe fell on the king's burden for unity. "Since . . . you have not kept my covenant and my decrees . . . I will most certainly tear the kingdom away from you," God promised (1 Kings 11:11). Not long after that, Jeroboam—one of Solomon's most trusted warriors—rebelled against the king. Though the nation didn't split until after Solomon died, God informed Solomon in advance that his dream of unity would be crushed. Sure enough— Solomon's heir was left with only two tribes of Jews. Jeroboam took the majority of subjects and formed a separate monarchy to the north.

● *Foreign adversaries.* As a consequence of Solomon's sin, God heated up cold wars with old foes of Israel. Two soldiers who had unsuccessfully clashed with King David—Hadad and Razon—were hot on the trail of revenge. The Bible doesn't describe any skirmishes between Israel and the two marauding bands of outlaws, but you get the idea that their harassment kept Solomon and his advisers from getting a good night's sleep.

● *Despair and heartache.* Perhaps the most sobering outcome of Solomon's self-indulgence was personal boredom and emptiness. Contrary to what you might think, life lost its luster for him. The pleasures of fame, money, and sex didn't have staying power. Solomon's description of their long-range impact on his life belongs on the marquee of every X-rated theater, and the package of every illegal drug: "I refused my heart no pleasure. . . . I surveyed all that my hands had done and . . . everything was meaningless, a chasing after wind; nothing was gained under the sun" (Ecclesiastes 2:10-12).

I've talked to teens who claim that their defiance of God's laws hasn't caused them a minute's pain. Maybe they're telling the truth. But I wonder: what will they write in *their* journals a few years down the road?

Solomon had the "good life" by the tail—and it bit him! I came across the following story in Charles

Swindoll's book, *Living on the Ragged Edge* (Word).
Note its irony:

> E. Stanley Jones . . . talks about a fictional
> person who lived out a fantasy life. All he had to
> do was think of it and (poof!) it happened. So
> this man . . . imagines a mansion and (poof!) he
> has a fifteen-bedroom mansion, three stories
> with servants instantly available to wait upon
> his every need.
>
> Why, a place like that needs several fine cars.
> So he again closes his eyes and imagines the
> driveway full of the finest wheels money can
> buy. And (poof!) there are several of the best
> vehicles instantly brought before his mind's
> eye. He is free to drive them himself, or sit way
> back in the limousine with that mafia glass
> wrapped around the rear, and have the chauf-
> feur drive him wherever he wishes.
>
> There's no other place to travel so he comes
> back home and wishes for a sumptuous meal
> and (poof!) there's the meal in front of him with
> all of its mouth-watering aromas and beauty—
> which he eats alone. And yet . . . there was
> something more he needed to find happiness.
>
> Finally, he grows so terribly bored and un-
> challenged that he whispers to one of the atten-
> dants, "I want to get out of this. I want to cre-
> ate some things again. I'd rather be in *hell* than
> be here." To which one of the servants replies
> quietly, "Where do you think you are?"

Let's not kid ourselves. The things that tempted Solomon—and us!—feel good at first. Otherwise, they
wouldn't entice us. But the "if-it-feels-good-do-it" philosophy of life has a flip side. It's called hell on earth.

3

THE THERMOMETER
OF THE HEART

Charles Kuralt is a CBS news reporter, noted for exploring Americana while crisscrossing the country in his van. In his travels, Kuralt has become convinced of this: Americans love to exaggerate. He was surprised by all the yarn spinners who are willing to look you right in the eye and tell you a whopper—particularly when talk turns to the weather.

When he asked a Nebraska farmer about hot summers in the plains, the farmer replied, "I don't think there's any place hotter. Farmers around here feed their chickens cracked ice so they won't lay hard-boiled eggs. And down by the river, it'll get so dry that the catfish will come up to the house and get a drink at the pump."

Another Nebraska farmhand told how low the river gets during a drought. "Frogs grow up to be three and four years old without ever having learned to swim," he insisted.

Yet the farm anecdotes paled in comparison to a report Kuralt heard in Maine. A resident gave the following account of a heat wave: "It was so hot here last summer that one day, right in the middle of corn season, corn started to pop. There was a herd of cows grazing next to the cornfield and they saw the popcorn coming down. And cows are not very bright, of course. They thought it was snow. Every one of them idiot cows stood there and froze to death."

Not all the weather whoppers focus on the heat, though. Another Maine resident said it was so cold one winter that "the words froze right in our mouths. We had to wait till spring to find out what we'd been talking about all winter." (From "Weather Whoppers," *Reader's Digest*, August 1986. Condensed from *On the Road with Charles Kuralt*, Putnam Publishing Group, 1985.)

We get a rib-tickling delight out of all the hot air in this country. But just as easily as words can spawn the healing effect of laughter, they can break the human heart. For every harmless "weather whopper" that spews from our lips, we launch scores of verbal missiles that wreak havoc with relationships. Who hasn't bled after getting in the way of a slashing tongue? Perhaps you still have scars from the last time somebody fired verbal salvos at you.

According to one estimate, we babble between 25,000 and 30,000 words every day. Multiply that figure by the billions of people in the world, and . . . *I don't even want to think about it!*

Over 100 references to the tongue dot the Book of Proverbs. Those verses mention the positive as well

as the damaging effects of words. Meditate on Prov
erbs 18:21: "The tongue has the power of life and
death." In this chapter, I'll concentrate on sins of the
tongue. The next chapter balances the scale by examining the positive side of speech.

What speech defects does Proverbs condemn?
What are the most obvious symptoms of foot-in-
mouth disease? What destructive consequences do
we often leave in the wake of careless words? How
can we put a leash on our runaway mouths and mini-
mize the damage?

The following pages beam the spotlight on these
questions. Fasten your seatbelts, and journey with
me through the "tongue" passages of Proverbs.

Lying Lips

God says that He loathes lies. Creating a false impression with words is one of the six things the Lord
expressly hates (Proverbs 6:16-17). The *King James
Version* of Proverbs 12:22 says that to mislead someone on purpose is "an abomination to the Lord" —
which is another way of saying He's disgusted with it.
Lying lips have a boomerang effect on us because "a
false witness will not go unpunished, and he who
pours out lies will not go free" (19:5). Without pulling
punches, God orders us to "put away from you a
deceitful mouth" (4:24 NASB).

What matters to God is the motive which propels
our words. Lying is not only relaying something we
know is untrue. It's also choosing words that cause
the hearer to believe something that isn't so.

In response to his parents' questions, Greg told
them, "I came home after school today." What he
didn't tell them was that he had first gone to the lake
with his friends. He had entered the house just minutes before his parents arrived home from work. "I

told the truth," he figured. "I *did* come home after school today. I just didn't say what *time* it was." Yet his carefully crafted reply gave his folks the wrong impression. They thought he had zipped straight home from school. Greg's choice of words didn't erase his *intent* to deceive.

Why do we stretch the truth? To make ourselves look more acceptable to others, or to receive benefits we couldn't claim otherwise. Yet a person who knows Jesus Christ can't lie and enjoy the apparent benefits. To deceive grieves the Holy Spirit, who calls the hearts of believers home. Part of the punishment for lying that's promised in Proverbs comes in the form of a joy-sapping twinge of guilt. As one psychologist put it, "Most people feel guilty because they are!"

Believe me, I learned the hard way that lying doesn't pay. The following incident occurred when I was a part-time youth director at a church. Though it took place when I was in grad school—back before the earth's crust hardened—it illustrates the inner turbulence that deceit causes.

"Did you ask your friend if he could sing for us at the banquet?" Jack asked me just before the worship service began.

"Uh—I talked to him Friday," I answered, fidgeting. "He's behind in his studies because he returned late from vacation. He said he'd better not make any more commitments right now."

Jack nodded. "Thanks a lot for asking him," he said, returning to his seat. I stared blankly at the bulletin in my hand, bewildered. I had lied. I *had* talked to my friend the week before, but I had forgotten to ask him about singing at the banquet. Something inside would not let me admit my failure to Jack.

There I was: the church youth director, devoted to full-time Christian service, squirming in my seat, too upset to even sing a hymn. A few years ago I probably wouldn't have given it another thought. But now my life had been surrendered to God. His Holy Spirit was convicting me. By the time the sermon began, the weight of the guilt was more than I could bear. I left my seat, tiptoed to where Jack sat, and motioned him outside. There I admitted my lie and asked his forgiveness ("How to Lie without Really Trying," *Freeway*, Spring 1973).

Confessing to Jack was not an easy thing to do. But to my surprise, his respect for me mushroomed rather than diminished. Though I felt lower than a snake's belly in a wagon rut, at least I modeled how to handle a lie.

Sleazy Slander

How does God feel about a slanderer? Look at Proverbs 10:18: "Whoever spreads slander is a fool." Maybe He's blunt on this issue because of the disastrous effect slander has on relationships. In the *New American Standard Bible*, Proverbs 16:28 says: "A slanderer separates intimate friends."

If you check the definition in a dictionary, you get the idea that "slander" refers only to *false* oral statements which ruin a person's reputation. It appears to be a specific form of lying that mars a third party's image. But *Webster's Dictionary* isn't our inspired source; Proverbs is. And the biblical word we translate "slander" has a different shade of meaning. The Hebrew word includes *true* as well as false remarks. No one explains the term better than Carole Mayhall in her book *Words That Hurt, Words That Heal* (NavPress):

In the Old Testament the word *slander* was used for bad reports in general. The Hebrew word meaning "to defame or strip one of his positive reputation" was used in the account of Joseph's true but "bad report" to his father concerning the wickedness of his brothers (Genesis 37:2). The same word was used in Numbers 13:32, the account of the ten spies who brought back a negative report about the Promised Land.

In the New Testament, the word for slander is comprised of two words, one meaning "against" and the other meaning "to speak." A slanderer, then, is simply one who speaks against another. Slander is the *open, intentional sharing of damaging information* and is characterized by bad reports that blemish or defame a person's reputation *whether they are true or not!*

Here's the bottom line: just because it's true doesn't mean we should announce it over a public address system. Before we add juicy tidbits to a conversation about somebody, let's apply the guidelines in Ephesians 4:29—"Do not let any unwholesome talk come out of your mouths, but only what is helpful for building others up according to their needs, that it may benefit those who listen." Unless we heed those conversational criteria, our gossipy chat becomes nothing more than "acid indiscretion."

"Tasteful" Talk

Another symptom of mouth disease detected by the probing X rays of Proverbs is hasty or impulsive speech—exercising the lips without activating the brain. Proverbs 12:18 compares rash speech to the piercing of a sword. Solomon also denounced the tendency to give a verbal reply before hearing all the facts, as in Proverbs 18:13: "He who answers before listening—that is his folly and his shame." Nobody with loose lips gets voted "Most Likely to Succeed." "Do you see a man who speaks in haste? There is more hope for a fool than for him" (29:20).

An article in *The State,* a Columbia, South Carolina newspaper, showed how impulsive words can be difficult to digest. Harvey Driggers was a radio announcer at WSCQ in Columbia. Several years ago, he and another man, Gene McKay, were chatting flippantly over the air about hypothetical situations. Out of the blue, McKay popped this question: "Would you eat a bowl of live crickets for $40,000?"

"Well, yes," Driggers answered.

"For $4,000?" McKay prompted.

"Yes," insisted Driggers.

"How about $150?" McKay inquired.

"No," Driggers replied.

Finally, Driggers conceded that he'd eat a bowl of crickets for as low as $250. The two were chuckling about the "Harvey Driggers Cricket Eating Fund" when phones began ringing. Unsolicited pledges of money for the fund flooded in. Listeners put their money where Driggers' mouth was! Before long, local officials provided a widely publicized public forum for the cricket-eating event. Days later, hundreds of onlookers gawked as Driggers poured chocolate over a bowl of live crickets and gobbled them down.

Driggers would be the first to vouch for the moral of this story: When we're forced to eat our words, they can be hard to stomach!

Taxing Tone

How we say something often packs more wallop than *what* we say. Perhaps more than any other tongue problem, a harsh tone of voice rips and tears like shrapnel in the hearer's heart. When we turn the volume of our voice up too high, others merely plug their ears and go on the defensive. "A gentle answer turns away wrath, but a harsh word stirs up anger" (15:1).

Experts tell us that of all the thoughts and feelings we communicate in a conversation:

- 7 percent is communicated by the actual words we say;
- 38 percent is transmitted by *how* we deliver those words (tone of voice);
- 55 percent is conveyed by nonverbal cues (gestures, facial expressions, etc.).

Imagine—our tone of voice carries five times more comfort or hurt than our choice of words!

A disturbing tone of voice usually stems from the soil of anger. Proverbs acknowledges the inevitable conflicts among people. That's why Solomon advises us to put a muzzle over our mouths whenever we're upset. "Drop the matter before a dispute breaks out" (17:14). "It is to a man's honor to avoid strife, but every fool is quick to quarrel" (20:3).

Vexing Voice

The final tongue problem we'll examine in the pages of Proverbs is hinted at by a drab, gray tombstone in an old English churchyard. The faint etchings reveal this epitaph:

BENEATH THIS STONE, A LUMP OF CLAY,
LIES ARABELLA YOUNG,
WHO, ON THE TWENTY-FOURTH OF MAY,
BEGAN TO HOLD HER TONGUE.

(as quoted in *Growing Strong in the Seasons of Life,* by Charles Swindoll, Multnomah Press).

What does Proverbs say about talking too much? "When words are many, sin is not absent, but he who holds his tongue is wise" (10:19). What are the consequences of wordiness? "He who guards his lips guards his soul, but he who speaks rashly will come to ruin" (13:3).

To put it another way, we "save face" by keeping the lower half shut! Former Senator Ed Muskie echoed the sentiment of Proverbs when he said, "Do not speak unless you can improve the silence." I'm not suggesting that you turn into a quiet wallflower. The point is *control,* not a squirt of Super Glue between your lips.

The matter of control reminds me of James 3:8: "No man can tame the tongue." Did James mean that it's useless to try to change our conversational habits? Is a diseased mouth terminal? No. If taming the tongue were impossible, God wouldn't hold us responsible for our words. Yet He does. Jesus Himself said, "Men will have to give account on the day of judgment for every careless word they have spoken" (Matthew 12:36). James' point is this: we can't lick tongue problems on our own apart from supernatural reinforcements.

How do you call on these reinforcements? If you're serious about winning the war against wayward words, heed the following battle strategies:

Oral Hygiene

1. If the light of Proverbs has exposed any form of sinful speech, confess it to God. To "confess" something simply means to agree with God's assessment of it. Overcoming a destructive verbal habit begins by admitting it's wrong. Whenever the Holy Spirit pricks our conscience over a remark, we can choose one of two responses: stubbornly carry the burden of guilt ourselves or confess it to Jesus and forget about it. "If we confess our sins, He is faithful and just and will forgive us our sins and purify us from all unrighteousness" (1 John 1:9).

2. Yield control of your tongue to God on a daily basis. A single prayer of confession gets us off on the right foot. Yet watching what we say must become a lifestyle. Shooting one prayer to heaven won't immunize us to the germs of a diseased tongue. David recognized that we must take the antidote in regular doses for the rest of our lives. His words in Psalm 39:1 acknowledge the continuing process that's involved: "I will watch my ways and keep my tongue from sin."

3. Give the Holy Spirit something to work with by memorizing Scripture. One high school student I know remarked, "There's just one bad thing about the Bible. It's almost never with me when I need it most!" He was referring to situations at school when he was about to blow his top and needed a relevant truth from Scripture to keep him calm. A solution is to memorize verses from the Bible. If your lips are sore from too much exercise, start with two verses previously quoted in this chapter: Proverbs 10:19 and Ephesians 4:29. Put the verses on note cards where you'll see them every day: by the phone, on a bulletin board, or inside a notebook.

4. Seek a prescription for the root problem, not just for the symptoms. Wayward words are a symptom of a deeper malady. They reveal an infected heart. In his book *Be Mature*, Warren Wiersbe tells about a professing Christian "who got angry on the job and let loose with some oaths. Embarrassed, he turned to his partner and said, 'I don't know why I said that. It really isn't in me.' But his partner wisely replied, 'It had to be in you or it couldn't have come out of you.' " Jesus stressed the same point. "The good man brings good things out of the good stored up in his heart, and the evil man brings evil things out of the evil stored up in his heart. *For out of the overflow of his heart his mouth speaks"* (Luke 6:45, italics mine).

How do you determine if an infection plagues your body? Pop a thermometer in your mouth. If the mercury zooms to 100-plus, you know you've been invaded by hostile germs. Body temperature is a so-called "vital sign of health." How can you tell if you're sick spiritually? Look at your conversational patterns through the lens of Scripture. The tongue is "the thermometer of the heart."

This closing perspective suggests that putting a rein on voice vices, as well as harnessing the tongue's positive potential, is impossible without a growing relationship with Jesus Christ. Sometimes we launch quickie prayers up to Jesus, asking for self-control and patience in our speech, without exhibiting a gut-level desire to know Him better. Yet Christlike qualities don't come packaged separately. They're a by-product of a love relationship with Him. Ways we cultivate that relationship include regular times of prayer, Bible study, and rubbing elbows with other Christians.

A simple rhyme from the pen of an American journalist, William Norris (quoted in Swindoll's *Growing Strong in the Seasons of Life*), sums up what Proverbs says about controlling our conversations:

> If your lips would keep from slips,
> Five things observe with care:
> To whom you speak, of whom you speak;
> And how, and when, and where.

4

THE MIGHTY
MOUTH

Sports personalities are often champions off the field too. When it comes to making garbled or muddled comments, they usually come in first place. A Hall of Fame baseball catcher and manager, Yogi Berra is still the king of confusing observations. "Ninety percent of baseball is half mental," he once asserted. A teammate, Bobby Richardson, wondered why Yogi carried so much life insurance. "Gee, Bobby, you don't know nothing about money," snapped Berra. "I'll get it all back when I die."

While they were enjoying lunch in a New York restaurant, Berra said to Richardson, "Don't look now, but somebody famous is sitting behind you."

"Who is it?" Richardson inquired.

"I'm not sure," Yogi answered. "I get them confused. There are two of them, brothers. One died. I'm not sure which one that is behind you, the one that died or the other one."

Curt Young had his moments too. The former Oakland A's pitcher, after serving up a Herculean home run to Reggie Jackson, observed, "He really jumped on it. He hit it a lot farther than it went." And here's how Bo Belinsky, another major league hurler, explained a string of successful outings: "Right now I feel that I've got my feet on the ground as far as my head is concerned."

Baseball players don't own the franchise on fuzzy remarks, though. Any lineup of verbal All-Stars would have to include Bill Peterson, former Florida State University and Houston Oilers football coach. In a terse reply to fans who second-guessed him, he said, "I'm the football coach around here, and don't you remember it!" He had his more solemn moments too. Before an important game, Peterson asked the Florida State captain to "please lead us in a few words of silent prayer" (From a column by Herman Helms, *The State* newspaper, Columbia, S.C., 27 March 1988).

Despite those offbeat comments from the lips of sports figures, the tongue really is a marvel of creation. Though it's the world's smallest but largest troublemaker, as illustrated in the last chapter, the tongue can also offer welcome words.

Giving Others a Jump

Rivet your attention to the following excerpts from Proverbs. In your own words, to what positive purpose of speech do they refer?

"An anxious heart weighs a man down, but a kind word cheers him up" (12:25).

"A tongue that brings healing is a tree of life" (15:4).

"Pleasant words are a honeycomb, sweet to the soul and healing to the bones" (16:24).

These verses zero in on the capacity of words to encourage or lift the spirits of others. New Testament references piggyback on this point from Proverbs. As far as the Apostle Paul was concerned, vocal encouragement is a *command,* not an option, among Christians. "Encourage one another, and build each other up" (1 Thessalonians 5:11).

Virgil Vogt employs a modern-day analogy to illustrate this ministry of the mouth:

The New Testament Greek word for encouragement contains the idea of being called alongside another. On the coldest winter days we do this to some of our cars. When one battery is so weak that it cannot spark its engine, we bring another car alongside and connect the working battery with heavy jumper cables to the weaker battery. Nothing is changed in the car that won't start. But with the direct infusion of power from the other vehicle, the weakness is overcome and the stranded car is able to function on its own.

We Christians often need to connect with the strength in others in order to get started or to keep going in difficult circumstances. We need someone to come alongside and give us a "jump" ("The Encouragement Connection," *New Covenant Magazine*).

When the energy oozes out of the batteries of people around you, how can you infuse them with power to keep going? You give others a jump when you:

- compliment a character trait or course of action you've observed in them.
- tell them how they encouraged you spiritually.
- say taken-for-granted things such as "I'm your friend," "I'm willing to listen," or "I care about you."
- defend them against unfair criticism.
- call to find out why they missed school or church.
- pray with them over a need they've expressed.
- share an answer to prayer, or a helpful insight God has shown you from the Bible.
- describe the vacancy they'd leave in your life if they were no longer around.

A Plea for Praise

A first cousin to encouragement is expressing appreciation. When someone else meets a need or fills a vacuum in your life, do you thank him or her for the contribution to your joy? In the last chapter of Proverbs, the writer lists the chores and characteristics of a godly wife and mother. He then describes the reaction of her family members. "Her children rise up and bless her; her husband also, and he praises her, saying: 'Many daughters have done nobly, but you excel them all' " (31:28-29, NASB).

Dad and the kids didn't just *feel* grateful—they voiced their appreciation. They unlocked the private vault where feelings were stored, and enriched her life through praise. We can't tiptoe around their example. Let's convert warm, fuzzy thoughts about people into words. Our legitimate praise may catapult them even closer to their potential as persons.

Back in college, I spotted a cartoon in a magazine. The cartoon simply showed a tombstone. Etched on the tombstone were these words:

THE MIGHTY MOUTH

**HERE LIES A MAN WHO WAS ALWAYS "GOING TO" . . .
NOW HE'S GONE.**

Every time I'm tempted to put off speaking a word of gratitude or appreciation, that epitaph surfaces in my mind. It reminds me that opportunities to exercise this ministry of the tongue are limited. Before I know it, a long-distance move — or even death — could bury the chance to say what's on my heart. Is there anyone to whom you owe gratitude, or to whom you've intended to pay a compliment? I'm not trying to be morbid, but after a friend or relative dies, it's too late to voice our appreciation. Neither a warm verbal eulogy nor an expensive wreath of flowers can make up for gratitude left unspoken during his or her liftime. After all, *no one can smell the flowers on his own coffin!*

Input and Output

Stuart Briscoe spoke the words almost two decades ago, in an address to the student body at Wheaton College. And yet every time I glean a new insight from a book, a Sunday School class, or devotions, those words come back to me and goad me into action. They keep me from becoming selfish about what I learn. What did he say that holds me accountable even today?

God never teaches you solely for your own benefit.

Briscoe was saying that we're supposed to pass along to others the spiritual truths we come across. Solomon would agree. Proverbs makes it clear that God designed our tongues as tools for teaching. "The lips of the righteous feed many, but fools die for lack of understanding" (10:21, NASB). The point is reinforced later. "The lips of the wise spread knowledge, not so the hearts of fools" (15:7). Proverbs 20:15

describes the priceless nature of talk that teaches when it says, "There is gold, and an abundance of jewels; but the lips of knowledge are a more precious thing" (NASB).

Does this mean God expects you to get a seminary degree and stand behind a lectern teaching for the rest of your life? No. Proverbs isn't referring to "teaching" in just a public, formal sense. And you don't need an ordination certificate on the wall before you can share truth from God's Word. Your tongue teaches whenever you:

- tell a friend or relative how to become a Christian.
- recount to members of your youth group an example of God's faithfulness to you.
- recite within earshot of others what the speaker said during your last youth group retreat.
- explain a Bible lesson to kids during children's church or Vacation Bible School.
- share an encouraging truth uncovered during your personal Bible reading.
- explain how a truth or verse from the Bible helped you make a decision.
- read aloud a Bible storybook when you're baby-sitting.

That's the nonprofessional kind of teaching Paul had in mind when he wrote, "Let the word of Christ dwell in you richly as you teach and admonish one another with all wisdom" (Colossians 3:16). There's only one qualification for teaching: regular exposure to God's truth. If you're learning, you have something to say.

Recently, I spotted a photo in a newspaper that reminded me to balance the input I'm getting with output. The Associated Press photo showed a muscular 32-year-old Britisher pulling a Concorde jet at London's Heathrow Airport. The strong man in the picture is David Gauder. He pulled the Concorde a total of 40 feet. According to the caption, Gauder has also pulled a 40-ton tractor-trailer, halted powerboats, and prevented two small aircraft from taking off—by strapping one to each arm!

The accompanying article described the eating habits of the 5'7", 240-pound Achilles. Gauder's *daily* diet consists of twenty-five eggs, five pounds of bananas, a whole chicken, six pints of milk, several baked potatoes, and two 32-ounce steaks. Just digesting that much food takes a lot of effort!

Despite his calorie intake, Gauder is a model physical specimen. But imagine what he'd look like if he ate all that food without regularly working out. In no time, flab would replace his rock-hard muscle.

Similarly, when we taste a steady diet of Bible truth, yet keep it to ourselves, we eventually become spiritually weak and flabby. The only way to burn off the calories and keep our spiritual figures trim is to exercise our lips. Sharing God's Word with others is like converting calories into energy. In the spiritual as well as the physical realm, the principle is inescapable: *health requires a balance between input and output.*

Verbal Gifts

Proverbs 22:11 salutes the individual "whose speech is gracious." To speak graciously means to give verbal gifts even when the recipients don't deserve them. It's treating the person to whom or about whom we're talking better than they've treated us. Another verbal exercise Solomon recommends is a well-timed word. "A man finds joy in giving an apt reply—and how good is a timely word" (15:23). "A word aptly spoken is like apples of gold in settings of silver" (25:11). Speaking a well-timed word requires sensitivity to the needs of people around us, and an awareness of their teachable moments. It's allowing their nonverbal cues to tell us when to turn the ignition to the motors in our mouths.

During my senior year of high school, my English teacher spoke some well-timed words. I didn't think much of myself at the time. I considered myself the type of person who could brighten up any room — by *leaving it,* if you know what I mean! I didn't like to study (as my report cards showed), and I had no intention of going to college.

Enter Mrs. Spratt. One day she found a poem I had written and left lying on my desk. What a shock it was when she began class the next day by reading it aloud! Then, in front of twenty classmates, she turned to me and predicted: "I can see it now. In a few years, you'll earn a degree in journalism. And someday the rest of us will read the poems and books you write. I'm not going to let you waste this God-given ability!"

Her words spawned a 180-degree turnaround in me. After that incident, I put more effort into school — especially English assignments. I cracked the books more often to please the first person who ever believed in me. Eventually, her prophecies about my journalism degree and writing career were fulfilled.

Conversation under Construction

A trowel is a tool with a handle and a flat, sharp-pointed blade. Bricklayers use it to spread mortar between bricks. Whoever invented the trowel obviously designed it for a *constructive* purpose, but you could use it to damage property or to hurt somebody.

When I wonder why God gave us tongues, I remember the trowel. Both the trowel and the tongue can slash a person to pieces. Yet both were created for the purpose of building up, not tearing down.

There's a trowel in your mouth. How are you using it?

5

THE FUTURE
IN PRESENT TENSE

've watched people make some foolish choices in my time. I've even made a few of my own. Yet the judgments handed down in the following court cases deserve top ranking in the "Absurd Decisions" category. I don't know if the presiding judges and juries had cobwebs in their craniums, but something obstructed the normal flow of their brain juices. Believe it or not . . .

- In New York City, a man tried to commit suicide by jumping into the path of a subway train. Though badly injured, he survived. Then he sued the subway authority and collected $650,000 in damages!

- When a man tried to rob a school, he fell through a skylight. He sued the school district over the injuries. The district's insurance company had to dish out

$260,000, plus $1,500 per month indefinitely.

● A drunk driver caromed off a curb and plowed into a telephone booth. The person in the phone booth at the time sustained injuries. So who did California's chief justice hold responsible for the accident? The company that designed the telephone booth!

● Two men needed a trimmer for the hedge that separated their lots. One of them bought a lawn mower from Sears. The neighbors lifted the lawn mower and actually tried using it, instead of a hedge trimmer, to cut the shrubbery. The heavy mower slipped from their grasp, and the blade slashed two fingers from one man's hand. Were they embarrassed for using a push mower in such a foolish fashion? Nope. The injured man sued Sears for *not* telling him that the machine was *not* a hedge cutter. He won a large monetary settlement (From the "Focus On The Family" newsletter, 24 February 1986).

Sounds like somebody trimmed the common sense off the minds of those decision makers. A little wisdom would've gone a long way to insure justice in those cases.

Even if you're never selected for jury duty or required to preside over a courtroom trial, you need to know how to make sensible choices. The pace of change in your life is rapidly accelerating. Over the next few years, your decision-making ability will be put to the test. Major matters such as selecting a college, picking a career, and deciding on a marriage partner will occupy your mind (not to mention the daily barrage of decisions related to things like social activities and relationship conflicts). When the time comes, I hope you'll exercise better judgment than the decision makers in the previously cited lawsuits. One way to increase your likelihood of making sound judgments is to digest what Proverbs says about the decision-making process. In this chapter we're going to examine four specific decision-making principles illustrated in Proverbs.

Who Owns Your Future?

The insight required for smart decisions isn't dispensed like prescriptions across a drugstore counter. Whether or not we exercise sound judgment depends a lot on whom or what we consult for help. Do we rely on our own wits or do we plug into divine discernment?

Decision-making principle #1 is: *The most reliable source of wisdom needed for making sensible choices is God.* That's not to say that an unbeliever who never cracks open a Bible or mutters a prayer can't make a right decision now and then. Within every human being God has created some degree of common sense. Yet, the know-how needed for a consistent pattern of sane choices comes from an ongoing relationship with our Creator. The closer we are to Him, the more we're apt to think and to react like Him—to view alternatives through the 20/20 lens of His Word.

Employing God as our primary consultant requires us to offer our future to Him—with no strings attached. Those who fully give God their future discover that they get back a more purposeful and adventuresome version of it. Other perspectives on decision-making from Proverbs won't make sense unless God has ownership of our lives. "Commit to the Lord whatever you do," Solomon advised, "and your plans will succeed" (16:3). Have *you* made a rational commitment of your future to the Lord? Have you given Him an OK to design the blueprint for your tomorrow? Tapping into God's wisdom requires transferring the deed to our life over to Him. Only then will we view each separate decision on the basis of how it fits into the big picture of His will. Only then will we make regular appointments with Him as a means of discovering His perspective on things. The *New American Standard Bible* says, "Those who seek the Lord understand all things" (28:5).

Wisdom is a by-product of personal integrity. When tough choices confront us, we can trust our intuition a lot more if we're living close to God. Proverbs 11:3 tells us, "The integrity of the upright guides them."

As spiritual as all this sounds, trusting your future to the Lord isn't something that comes naturally. God's plans may conflict with yours once in a while. To relinquish complete control of the future to God is gut-wrenching for some people. Can you identify with the following poem? I wrote it back in college as I faced decisions about my future.

Trust you with my life?
God, that's the same as saying,
"Here, it's yours now."
And I'm not sure I'm ready for that.
I'm afraid to say, "You take over, God."
It's risky.
What will happen to my plans?
I have my own ideas about
who to date
where to go
how to spend my time and money
what to do after graduation.
I want to be sure
before I give my life away
that You won't spoil things for me.
God, if I trust You with my life,
What would You do with it?

My poem—which was actually a prayer—illustrates that learning to trust God with our future is a *process*, not an instantaneous occurrence. Doubts and honest questions are a legitimate part of the process. God doesn't reject us when we question Him because He knows that we're interested in at least considering His claim on our lives. May the end result of your inquiry be summarized by Proverbs 3:5-6: "Trust in the Lord with all your heart and lean not on your own understanding; in all your ways acknowledge Him, and He will make your paths straight."

Thinking in the Future Tense

Centuries ago a small band of Roman invaders landed on the shores of what is now England. Defenders of the island had successfully repelled previous attempts by other groups to wrest away control of the area. When the defenders first spotted the new invaders, they strutted around confidently, figuring they could successfully repel another attempt. Then the natives witnessed a spectacle that changed their cocky attitude. What they saw melted their hearts and siphoned off their confidence. Before moving inland, the Roman soldiers burned every one of their own boats! Retreat was no longer an alternative. It was forward or die!

The Roman soldiers were "thinking in the future tense." With the goal of taking over the island in mind, they pondered this question: "What can we do *now* in order to increase the likelihood of success?" That's when they burned the boats. They knew they'd fight harder if escape wasn't an option.

This mode of planning illustrates **decision-making principle #2: Determine the effect future goals and needs should have on current choices.** I call this the art of "putting the future into the present tense." Our tendency is to bracket off the present from the future. We usually make choices based on current benefits rather than long-term consequences. But Proverbs makes it clear that reaching tomorrow's goals should affect the way we operate now. (After all, it wasn't raining when Noah began construction on the ark. But he knew he'd be in over his head if he waited until the first raindrop fell.)

Proverbs uses the ant, a hard-working son, and a housewife to show that effective decision-making requires "thinking in the future tense." First, the author compliments the ant for anticipating needs of the future, then taking the necessary steps in the present to meet those needs. "Go to the ant, you sluggard; consider its ways and be wise! It has no commander, no overseer or ruler, yet it stores its provisions in summer and gathers its food at harvest" (6:6-8). The author employs the same agricultural analogy to salute the diligence of a young man. "He who gathers crops in summer is a wise son, but he who sleeps during harvest is a disgraceful son" (10:5). Food on the table in January was dependent on a certain course of behavior in August.

The housewife portrayed in Proverbs 31 also made choices in the present based on her anticipation of the future. She could smile at the prospect of winter blizzards, because during short-sleeve weather she made scarlet overcoats for family members (31:21-22).

You may think that the illustrations in Proverbs are as out-of-date as the Hula-Hoop. After all, you don't think a lot about what you'll eat or wear six months down the road. But the point is timeless: *get in the habit of mulling over the present implications of your future needs and aspirations.*

Let's get specific. In a national survey, teens in the

United States indicated that choosing a college and career are their biggest concerns. Yet saving money for college isn't in vogue: 77 percent of the 742 teens surveyed say they've saved no money toward their future education. Their lack of savings, though, isn't due to a lack of resources. Most of the teens who responded work part-time, earning $50–$100 per week. They reported spending their money on clothes, stereos, movie tickets, and car expenses. ("Kids Fret Yet Don't Save For College," Mark May-field, *USA Today*, 18 June 1989)

Spending habits aren't necessarily a matter of right and wrong. Don't think Proverbs is advocating a miserly existence now as a way to bankroll the future. Yet don't miss the point: the teens reported worrying about funds for college, yet few of them put aside even a small portion of their earnings to increase the likelihood of their enrolling. That's enslavement to the present. They're aware of future needs, yet fail to make current choices in light of those needs. That kind of reasoning is as solid as quicksand.

Don't let *your* future become a time when you wish you'd have done what you aren't doing now. When you're dying of thirst, it's too late to think about digging a well.

Painful Presumption

Perhaps the greatest magician and escape artist of all time was Harry Houdini. His feats would have made even David Copperfield stand up and clap. Within seconds he could break out of any handcuff, straitjacket, or jail cell.

Except one. Officials of a jail in the British Isles outsmarted him. After being locked in the jail cell, Houdini toyed with the door lock for over two hours. He had picked similar locks in as little as three seconds. But nothing he tried worked. Finally, he gave up and slumped exhaustedly against the cell door. It swung open. The door to the jail cell had never been locked! (Paul Lee Tan, *Encyclopedia of 7700 Illustrations,* Assurance Publishers)

The normally shrewd escape artist *presumed* the cell door was locked, without investigating the matter. He took for granted that they wouldn't ask him to escape from a jail that was unlocked. He supposed a basic fact to be true without checking for proof.

Houdini's presumption illustrates **decision-making principle #3:** *Avoid hasty choices based primarily on presumption or subjective feelings and get all the facts you can to aid in the decision-making process.*

According to Proverbs 13:10, "Through presumption comes nothing but strife" (NASB). Presumption is proceeding on the basis of whim or emotion, apart from rational thought about the alternatives. It's assuming something is true, or will work out OK, without evidence or proof. In contrast to the person who presumes about the future, "every prudent man acts out of knowledge" (13:16), and a wise planner "acquires knowledge" (18:15). That's another way of saying that he gets all the information he can, and proceeds cautiously when choosing among alternatives. He doesn't beat around the bush when it's time to choose. Yet neither does he take a rash step without checking out the ground where his foot will land.

To transport this planning concept from theory to practice, let's look at some examples of presumptuous choices. Instead of researching the facts, the following people took too much for granted:

● Instead of buckling down academically, Greg went through his first three years of high school as if he were allergic to textbooks. His C– average was light years away from his potential. Yet he figured that a higher-than-average SAT score, combined with better grades his senior year, would get him into the college of his choice. He was quite surprised and discouraged when his application was rejected. In addition to presuming about his future, Greg failed to consider the effect future goals should have had on his current behavior and choices.

● When it came to members of the opposite sex, Ron, a staunch Christian, was determined to exercise high moral standards. When an R-rated movie came to the local cinema, he went to see it because it featured his favorite actor, and promised lots of hair-raising adventure. From past experiences, Ron knew he was vulnerable to lust when he was exposed to sex scenes, but he figured this particular movie was rated R based solely on violence. He was wrong. In the middle of the movie was a steamy bedroom scene. Ever since that night, Ron has struggled more with his thought life because of flashbacks to that erotic incident. He wouldn't have gone to the movie if he'd known it was so offensive. But finding out in advance about the sex scene would have been as simple as asking a few questions, or reading a review of the movie. Ron didn't acquire the information that was readily available.

● Jan skipped school on Friday. She assumed her science teacher wouldn't dish out homework for Monday. Though Jan was on the brink of failing science, she didn't call a classmate to find out for sure about homework. After all, Mrs. Bradley had never assigned homework over the weekend. You can probably guess the result: Jan got a zero on the first-ever weekend assignment in science class. Because her grade was so low, Jan should have asked a classmate to notify her about any potential assignments. Or she could have phoned someone after school on Friday. She made a decision based on past experience instead of checking on current facts.

● As a college freshman, Pete worked a part-time job. Since his freshman courses didn't require much studying, he was able to work twenty hours a week. Before enrolling for his sophomore year, he went into debt for a new car. He concluded that he made enough money from his part-time job to cover the monthly payment and insurance. What he didn't figure on, though, was a tougher slate of courses his sophomore year. The extra academic burden forced him to cut back on his part-time hours and put him in a financial squeeze. He ended up selling the car at a loss, because he had made a purchase choice rooted in presumption rather than the facts. Pete's decision to buy the car was based on the previous year's academic load. Before assuming such a large debt, he should have investigated the time requirements of the more complex sophomore courses.

These scenarios show that the heavenly advice from Proverbs is as down-to-earth as artificial turf on an athletic field. So before you reserve a dorm room at a university, visit the campus and uncover all the pluses and minuses. Take a list of questions to ask students you run into, as well as the administrators you meet. Don't assume anything unless you've substantiated it with research. And before you let anyone slip an engagement ring on your finger, make sure you have the lowdown on his character. If you wear his diamond because he looks like a matinee idol, figuring he'll change his bad habits after a trip to the altar, that's presumption. You'll get hitched to a heartache instead of a hunk.

Two Heads Are Better Than One

Susan cheated on Mr. Radford's algebra exam. That evening, badgered by guilt, she told her best friend

Rhonda about it. "A better grade isn't worth what I'm feeling now," Susan admitted. "I'm not sure what to do."

Rhonda was honest with her. "The conviction you're experiencing goes to show that a Christian can't sin and enjoy it for long. At least it's proof that you belong to Christ. There's only one thing you can do. Tell Mr. Radford."

"You've got to be kidding!" Susan said. "Mr. Radford isn't a Christian, but he knows I am. What will he think if I tell him I cheated?"

"That's beside the point," answered Rhonda. "You aren't responsible for his reaction. Only for yours. You know as well as I do that you've got to go through with it."

The next day, following Rhonda's advice, Susan confessed to Mr. Radford. "Please forgive me for what I did," she stammered. "I was worried about going on restriction if I flunked your course. But that's no reason to sacrifice my character."

After changing her grade, Mr. Radford said, "Susan, I've taught at this school for five years. You're not the only student who has ever cheated, but you're the first one who has come and asked forgiveness. You're the first example of a real Christian I've seen on campus!"

Don't expect folks to respond with warm fuzzies every time you try to set things straight. The point of Susan's episode is this: she received and acted on sound advice. Her actions illustrate *decision-making principle #4: As you proceed through the process of deciding or planning, get counsel from others.*

Jesus never intended for any of His followers to go it alone. That's why the New Testament uses terms like "family" and "body" to describe the church. From day one He planned for believers to relate closely to one another, and help each other along on the journey to maturity. "In Christ we who are many form one body, and each member belongs to all the others" (Romans 12:5).

Solomon made the same point hundreds of years earlier. Proverbs 17:17 salutes the value of a friend to support us and offer perspectives during trials. It says, "A friend loves at all times, and a brother is born for adversity." Staying sharp spiritually requires the kind of feedback Rhonda gave Susan. "As iron sharpens iron, so one man sharpens another" (27:17).

Whether or not we seek others' guidance has a lot to do with our future success. "Where there is no guidance, the people fall, but in abundance of counselors there is victory" (11:14, NASB). "Plans fail for lack of counsel, but with many advisers they succeed" (15:22). God has a name for the person who's too proud to seek advice. It's found in Proverbs 12:15: "The way of a *fool* seems right to him, but a wise man listens to advice" (italics mine).

Proverbs isn't telling you to rely on others' ideas to the point of becoming indecisive. Which summer job you select, which colleges you visit, whether or not you break up with a boyfriend or girlfriend — these decisions ultimately fall into *your* lap. Proverbs merely encourages you to rely on sources outside yourself to increase the likelihood of choosing wisely. If you give your future to God and ask Him for wisdom as needed (principle #1), consider the impact future goals and needs should have on current choices (principle #2), find out the facts so you'll know what you're getting into (principle #3), and obtain objective feedback from people you trust (principle #4), the odds of making right decisions are in your favor.

Of course, the caliber of counsel you receive depends on the quality of the person you consult. Trying to squeeze wisdom from a hollow mind is as frustrating as trying to put toothpaste back into the tube. No human being is right all the time, but the following guidelines can help you select an adviser.

• *What is the person's reputation?* Will he or she keep confidences? Do most people recognize this person's integrity and spiritual maturity? Is he or she secure enough to disagree with you or to tell you the truth even when it hurts?

• *What is his or her track record as a counselor?* How did previous advice given by this person work out? Do you rate him or her highly when it comes to common sense? What do friends who have consulted with this person say? (A counselor's best advertisement is a satisfied customer.)

• *What experience does this person have with the issue at hand?* Some dilemmas require specialized feedback. If you want the Bible's perspective on a decision, your adviser needs a working knowledge of God's Word. Call on a godly relative or your church's youth director. If you're wrestling with the choice of a college major or whether to accept a particular job opportunity, talk with someone who's older, who knows about those decisions.

• *How well does the person know you?* Does he or she have a handle on your strengths and weaknesses? Is he or she familiar enough with your past experiences, abilities, and goals to know how you'd react in various relational or employment contexts? If a person knows what makes you tick, he or she usually does a better job helping you sort out various alternatives.

The four insights we've examined in this chapter are not the only principles Proverbs offers about choosing or finding God's will. But it's enough to get you started. What counts isn't how much Bible content you take in, but how much you put into action.

6

COPING WITH CONFLICT

It happened in West Palm Beach, Florida. According to an Associated Press release, a 15-year-old girl who was stood up on prom night was trying to get even. She was suing her date for $49.53 — the cost of shoes, flowers, and hairdo which he never got to see.

Her date claimed he broke his ankle, and told her a week in advance that he couldn't go. She maintained that he stood her up without notice. The boy's mom offered to reimburse the money, but the jilted girl was pressing the issue in court. "She tells me the boy has to be punished," said his frustrated mom.

I don't know if breaking a date is sufficient grounds for a lawsuit, but the next story, clipped from *People* magazine, is definitely of the law-breaking variety. In the early 1980s, a pizza parlor owner in Allentown, Pennsylvania survived several attempts on his life. The person responsible for those attempts was his wife. First she hired an assailant to whack her husband over the head with a baseball bat. When the Louisville Slugger left him with nothing worse than a headache, she placed a trip wire at the top of the stairs. When that failed, she had him shot—*on two separate occasions.*

Before the first shooting, she drugged his chicken soup so he'd sleep soundly. Then, while he slept, a hired killer sneaked into his room, shoved a pistol against his head, and pulled the trigger. The pizza-maker needed more than aspirin to recover this time around, yet he survived. After he recuperated, his wife hired yet another gunman to shoot him in the chest. Miraculously, he suffered little damage. Yet more remarkable than his survival was his attitude when he discovered that his wife, together with her secret lover, was behind the attacks. He forgave her on the spot. He paid her attorney fees. After she was convicted of soliciting for murder, he visited her regularly in prison.

After four years behind bars, she moved back in with her husband. They say they're more in love than ever. (For his sake, let's hope so!) As he hugged his wife for a photographer, the bullet-riddled man said, "I don't understand why people break up over silly things!"

Few conflicts end up in court or result in attempted murder. Yet at any given time, most of us have at least one relationship that's out of kilter. Trying to get along with some people is as frustrating as wrestling with an octopus!

If the relational atmosphere in your house, classroom, or place of employment is as tense as a round of arms negotiations with the Soviets, take another excursion through the Book of Proverbs. Dotted throughout its chapters are time-tested principles for preventing or managing unhealthy forms of interpersonal conflict.

The Return of the World's Smallest but Largest Troublemaker

What is the number one manufacturer of strife between people? That's easy: *the tongue.* Chapters three and four in this book put the spotlight on the destructive and constructive power of words. Yet it's impossible to pinpoint what Proverbs says about handling conflict without referring once again to the damage caused by loose lips. ***Principle #1 for managing conflict*** is this: *Discipline your verbal habits and cultivate the fine art of listening.*

God doesn't beat around the bush on this issue. According to Proverbs 6:16-19, one of the seven things "that are detestable" to the Lord (v. 16) is one whose mouth "stirs up dissension among brothers" (v. 19). We stir up dissension when we speak to someone in a harsh tone of voice. "A gentle answer turns away wrath, but a harsh word stirs up anger" (15:1). We also do some stirring when we speak hastily without mulling over the possible consequences of our words. "Reckless words pierce like a sword" (12:18). No matter how good a Christian you are, you'll get angry once in a while; but a mature person taps the power of God and *thinks* about his response. "The heart of the righteous weighs its answers" (15:28).

When the temperature of a conversation nears the boiling point, perhaps the wisest way to cool things down is to zip our lips. Keeping quiet enables us to listen more attentively to the feelings and perspectives of others. Proverbs 18:2 employs contrast to show the importance of listening. "A fool finds no pleasure in understanding but delights in airing his own opinions." More directly, Proverbs 18:13 insists that "he who answers before listening—that is his folly and his shame."

Unless you really have a genuine concern about a relationship, controlling the tongue is an unrealistic goal. In her book *Real Friends: Becoming the Friend You'd Like to Have* (Harper & Row), Barbara Varenhorst explains how listening and caring go hand in hand. She discusses the concept of "listening with the heart":

> Heart listening can be learned, but it cannot be practiced or done mechanically. You can listen mechanically with your ears, but not with your heart. Why? Because the essence of listening with your heart is to put your whole self into trying to hear what the other is saying, because you care that much. Unless you care, you won't stop talking, resisting, or ignoring long enough to hear what is being said. You won't sacrifice your time or convenience to hear the other's feelings behind the words or twisted behaviors. If you care enough, you will learn the necessary skills, and then you will practice repeatedly, putting out the effort needed to learn to "listen with your heart."

If listening is so vital to preventing and resolving conflict, we need a tool to evaluate our listening habits. Mull over the eight questions that follow. As you read the questions, keep one person in mind who's important to you, but with whom you've had problems getting along lately. Then put a check mark by the appropriate answer.

ARE YOU A GOOD LISTENER?

1. When engaged in conversation with this person, do you find it difficult to keep your mind from wandering to other subjects?

Yes _____ No _____ Sometimes _____

2. When talking with this person, do you focus only on the facts being discussed and overlook the person's feelings?

Yes _____ No _____ Sometimes _____

3. Do certain words, phrases, mannerisms, or ideas make it more difficult for you to really hear this person?

Yes _____ No _____ Sometimes _____

4. When you are talking with this person, instead of listening, are you thinking of what you're going to say next?

Yes _____ No _____ Sometimes _____

5. If you feel it's going to take too much time to understand something this person is trying to explain to you, do you try to change the subject or finish off that particular conversation?

Yes _____ No _____ Sometimes _____

6. When this person is talking to you, do you try to make him or her think you are paying attention even though you're thinking of something else?

Yes _____ No _____ Sometimes _____

7. When you are listening to this person are you easily distracted by other sights and sounds?

Yes _____ No _____ Sometimes _____

8. As this person talks, does your "body language" inform him or her of your disinterest? Do you keep glancing at your watch? Do your eyes wander? Do you start walking backward while pretending to listen?

Yes _____ No _____ Sometimes _____

The *ideal* listener would have answered "No" to all eight questions. However, I've never run into a human being who is that close to perfection! Total up your responses. If you answered "Yes" to four or more of the questions, you have a listening problem. Ask the Lord to fit you with a "hearing aid" that will pick up more of the sound waves generated by this person's speech.

If you're currently on a collision course with a parent, an authority figure at school, or a peer, turn back a few pages to the chapter titled "The Thermometer of the Heart." As you review the symptoms of foot-in-mouth disease in chapter 3 and skim the practical strategies for winning the war against wayward words, ask the Lord to show you how the material relates to any hostile relationships you may be experiencing.

Whether or not you follow through on this tip depends on how badly you want the relationship restored. Even if you aren't to blame for the ill will, God may want to change the other person *by first changing you.*

Behind Enemy Lines

When we're in conflict with someone we *love,* we have motivation to negotiate our differences and resolve them. But what about when we're in conflict with people for whom we don't give a rip? Why should we care about the prospect of intimacy with someone we label an "enemy"? You know the people I'm referring to—the girl who talked a couple of your friends out of attending your party; the teacher who wouldn't believe your side of a story; the coach who wouldn't give you a fair shot at starting because your older brother had caused him problems; or the football-playing bully who thumps the back of your head in social studies class, egging you into a fight you couldn't possibly win.

During a sermon on "loving your enemies," a young man scribbled the following poem on the church bulletin:

I know you said,
"Love your enemies, and pray for those who persecute you" (Matthew 5:44).
But *how*, Lord?
That commandment makes me squirm in my seat.
It seems like "Mission Impossible" when I think of some people.
You know how
        cold
        critical
        haughty some folks are.
You know how Fred loves to put me down.
How Bill isn't satisfied unless he's beating me at something.
How Marie used me to get a date with my best friend.
Loving them is easier said than done, Lord.
I don't think I have it in me.

Can you identify with the young man? As you read his poem, whose face appeared on the dartboard of your mind? If there's someone you loathe, Proverbs has a timely, but tough-to-swallow word for you. *Conflict-managing insight #2* is this: *Treat enemies better than they deserve and trust God to avenge their mistreatment of you.*

You're probably thinking that it seems hypocritical to be nice to somebody you'd like to shove into the ring with Mike Tyson. God understands your feelings, yet He doesn't withdraw His advice. "If your enemy is hungry, give him food to eat; if he is thirsty, give him water to drink. In doing this, you will heap burning coals on his head, and the Lord will reward you" (Proverbs 25:21-22).

What does all this mean about "heaping burning coals" on an enemy's head? Does it mean that if we can't get our hands on chunks of coal, could we substitute a bucket of scalding water? *Whoa!* Before you get the idea that Proverbs is condoning torture, let's consult Charles Swindoll's book *Living Beyond the Daily Grind Book II* (Word) for a little background on this verse.

> In ancient days, homes were heated and meals were fixed on a small portable stove, somewhat like our outside barbecue grills. Frequently, a person would run low on hot coals and would need to replenish his supply. The container was commonly carried on the head. So as the individual passed beneath second-story windows, thoughtful people who had extra hot coals in their possession would reach out of the window and place them in the container atop his head. Thanks to the thoughtful generosity of a few folks, he would arrive at the site with a pile of burning coals on his head and a ready-made fire for cooking and keeping warm. "Heaping burning coals on someone's head" came to be a popular expression for a spontaneous and courteous act one person would voluntarily do for another.

Before you dismiss this warmhearted approach to enemies as an evidence of weakness, or as ivory-tower nonsense, let's see what else Proverbs says on the subject. Our next stop is at Proverbs 24:17. At first glance this verse seems to add to the unrealistic burden already dumped on you. "Do not gloat when your enemy falls; when he stumbles, do not let your heart rejoice." But then God adds an interesting comment: "Or the Lord will see and disapprove and *turn His wrath away from him* (24:18, emphasis mine).

Zoom in on that last phrase of verse 18. In some mysterious way, when we nurse a grudge or treat a foe rudely, God refuses to take His own vengeance out on the other person. When we fail to pray and release our resentment to God, we hinder the divine process and may actually prevent our enemy from experiencing negative consequences that God had in mind for him or her. Proverbs 20:22 says, "Do not say, 'I'll pay you back for this wrong!' Wait for the Lord, and He will deliver you." Centuries later, Paul expanded on the same point. "Do not repay anyone evil for evil. . . . As far as it depends on you, live at peace with everyone. Do not take revenge, my friends, but leave room for God's wrath, for it is written: 'It is mine to avenge; I will repay,' says the Lord. . . . Do not be overcome by evil, but overcome evil with good" (Romans 12:17-19, 21).

I'm aware that obeying this "love your enemy" concept is difficult. But obeying it is still easier than living with the harmful effects of resentment. Your only other option is a get-even attitude that, when ignored, acts like a cancerous tumor which turns a healthy body into a corpse. For your own sake, let God perform emergency surgery. If you're overwhelmed by the impossibility of sweetening your sour attitude toward someone who has hurt you, admit it to the Lord. No one has enough spirituality to resolve conflict with a foe unless God gives him an intravenous injection of power.

Gary learned the hard way that our time of greatest inadequacy is the moment when God intervenes. During a mile run at a district track meet, a competitor intentionally elbowed Gary on a far turn, away from the gaze of the high school officials. The bump forced Gary off the track for a few seconds—a move that *was* seen by an official. Despite protest by Gary's coach, Gary was disqualified from the race—an event he had a good chance of winning.

He had trained hard for the chance to win a medal, but his hopes were dashed by a cheating competitor and a track official who couldn't verify his account of the incident. Gary experienced an unhappy secret of existence on planet Earth: sometimes life is downright unfair! As a Christian, the incident posed a stiff test to Gary's faith. How would he react? Would he keep ranting and raving for weeks about a circumstance he couldn't change, or would he ventilate his anger in prayer and call on the Lord for help?

A long talk with his dad simmered Gary down a bit. Then a closed-door discussion with God over the unfairness of it all threw more cold water on the fires of resentment. I'm not saying that when friends consoled him the next day at school, he muttered, "Praise the Lord, anyhow!" The disqualification irked him. Yet the conversations with his dad and with God had the effect of successful chemotherapy treatment on the tumor of revenge.

Two weeks later, Gary was one of the favorites for the mile run in the state championships. A disqualification at the district level would normally keep an athlete out of the state meet, but an official protest over the controversial district meet got Gary reinstated. Who was his chief rival in the mile run? You guessed it—the Elbow Guy.

I wish this story had a fairytale ending. Like the 1924 Olympic race featuring Eric Liddell of *Chariots of Fire* fame. You know—the hero reaches the finish line first to the roar of the crowd. But Hollywood producers won't pay a dime for Gary's story. The guy who had previously elbowed Gary beat him by an eyelash—this time fair and square. Gary didn't feel like double-dating with the guy, nor making him his college roommate, but he did go out of his way to give the winner a congratulatory handshake.

Gary displayed something rare at the state championships. It's called "Christianity." He decided to play by God's rulebook for relationships, rather than the world's. Who was the real winner?

Response-Ability

Gary's reaction to injustice illustrates **conflict-managing principle #3** from Proverbs: *When someone sins against us, whether he's friend or foe, we're responsible for how we respond; and our first response should be forgiveness.*

When you put Proverbs 10:12 under the microscope, the idea of "responding responsibly" comes clearly into focus. Solomon used different terms, but he was advocating the same concept. "Hatred stirs up dissension, but love covers all wrongs." Later on he again salutes the value of forgiveness. "A man's wisdom gives him patience; it is to his glory to overlook an offense" (19:11).

By adding a verse from the New Testament to our inventory, we discover why God's insistence on forgiveness is reasonable. A few folks in the church at Colosse had trouble getting along. (Sound familiar?) Paul echoed the counsel from Proverbs. "Clothe yourselves with compassion . . . forgive whatever grievances you may have against one another. Forgive as the Lord forgave you" (Colossians 3:12-13).

Here's Paul's "bottom line": every Christian has an experiential basis for forgiving someone who's misused him. Everyone who has been on the receiving end of

God's forgiveness knows what it's like to be treated better than he deserves. That's why there's no excuse for failing to return the favor. God repaired our relationship with Him by modeling for us the way He wants us to treat others.

The three conflict-managing insights in this chapter don't exhaust what Scripture says about repairing broken relationships, but you've had enough to digest in one serving. As we close this chapter, keep this in mind — if you energetically apply these principles, there's no guarantee you'll salvage every relationship. The other person may not choose to play the game by God's rulebook. Yet over the long haul, in your relationships you'll experience more harmony than harm.

7

HOW TO HANDLE
A CRITIC

The coach's shrill whistle signaled the end of the first tennis practice of the season. Sandy grabbed her racket and jogged toward the other team members who were headed for the locker rooms. When she came within earshot of the group, she heard one of the new sophomore players ask, "How do you think we'll do this year, Eddie?"

Eddie, who had been an all-conference netter for the past two years, replied, "If my co-captain will spend more time on the practice court and less time with her boyfriend, and if some of you newcomers keep playing like you practiced today, we'll go a long way."

Their conversation shifted to another topic, but Sandy couldn't get her mind off Eddie's comment.

WISE UP

His words badgered her throughout the evening. Finally, she vented feelings in a note to Eddie.

Dear Eddie,

You and I have played tennis together and have been friends long enough that I feel I should write this note. I don't think you realized what it sounded like after practice today when you joked about Andrea needing to spend more time practicing and less time with her boyfriend. You and I know Andrea and what a hard worker she is. That's why we both voted for her as co-captain.

I know we teased her about Jeff always waiting for her after practice last year. And I expect you meant to be funny with what you said today. But your comment could have sounded pretty critical to the new members of the team who don't really know Andrea. The first impression they got about her from your words was that Andrea is too love-struck to concentrate on her tennis. And first impressions, even inaccurate ones, are tough to overcome.

I'm not meaning to condemn you for what you said; I've been guilty of the same kind of things lots of times. But I think as team leaders—people the new players respect and look up to—we have to be extra careful about making critical statements. We could easily prejudice people's opinions without meaning to at all.

I know you didn't mean anything by your comment today. But as a friend whom I respect a lot, I thought you would want to know how it could have sounded to someone else.

Thanks for listening,
Sandy

The next day, after Eddie read Sandy's note, he bristled. "I didn't mean any harm!" he reasoned. Yet deep down he knew Sandy's note had hit the bull's-eye. Before practice that afternoon, he apologized to Sandy. Eddie even thanked her for caring enough to write the note. And he made it a point to compliment Andrea in front of the new team members. Both Eddie and Sandy say that the incident strengthened the respect they felt for each other. (Adapted from "Nobody Loves a Critic," by Lew Allen, *Campus Life Magazine,* December 1978.)

If only all criticism were given and received in such a mature manner! Yet we're all aware that such "they-lived-happily-ever-after" conclusions are rare. Even when a situation calls for it, confrontation can cause friendships to fizzle or the flame of romance to flicker.

When someone you care about says or does something that's out of line, you owe it to yourself and to the other person to speak up. If you don't flush the negative feelings out of your system, a small irritation may turn into bitterness that ruins the relationship. In the same way, making honor roll in the school of Christian living requires passing a course on *receiving* criticism. We need people who are willing to shine the spotlight on dark spots in our character or behavior.

Calling All Critics

To "criticize" means to evaluate, or to act as a judge. Whether a critic is evaluating art, a teacher's competency, a new movie, or somebody's social skills at a party, he observes evidences, draws conclusions, and expresses them.

We tend to associate criticism with negative feedback. "Don't be so critical!" we say to someone who has the tendency to see the flaws in everything or everybody. But criticism can come in positive as well as negative forms. You're a *positive critic* when you identify a person's strengths or accomplishments. You judge a person's performance or behavior as satisfactory, or worthy of special commendation. ("I like the way you stood up for Susan when she wasn't here to defend herself." "I admire the way you stay after practice to work on free throws. It's easy to think that your success on the court just comes naturally.") This type of criticism is expected among Christians. Paul wrote, "Encourage one another and build each other up" (1 Thessalonians 5:11).

Yet positive feedback isn't the only kind we need. *Negative criticism* exposes unsatisfactory behavior or achievements. In using negative criticism, the critic spots a weakness or a mistake, and shines a verbal spotlight on it.

Sandy's letter to Eddie is an example of *constructive* negative criticism. When it's based on valid evidence, thorough analysis, concern for the other person, and expressed in a loving manner, negative criticism stretches the recipient and motivates him to change. After all, how can you strengthen a weakness or avoid a mistake that you're unaware of? Gordon MacDonald points out the value of negative criticism to spiritual growth:

> We all need truth-tellers, even if we don't really want them. Pass them up or avoid them, and our spiritual passion may be in great jeopardy. . . .
> Not many people want to *tell* the truth when it's painful, and not a lot of people want to *hear* the truth if it's painful. . . . But no one grows where truth is absent. No one is pushed *to be* and *to do* the best. When you look at this deficit from a Christian perspective, it describes a situation where men and women are never going to

become all that God has made them to be. . . .

One rarely grows without a rebuke. One solid and loving rebuke is worth a hundred affirmations. Rebukes are the purifiers which keep spiritual passion clear and forceful *(Restoring Your Spiritual Passion,* Oliver-Nelson.)

However, negative criticism can destroy as well as build up people. If based on hearsay, propelled by a selfish motive, or communicated in an insensitive manner, negative opinions can destroy a person's fragile self-esteem.

A wise critic will balance negative feedback with positive observations. And anyone who wants to cultivate Christlike character will welcome both types of criticism.

Critical Condition

Proverbs warns us against an "I-can-do-it-myself" approach to Christianity. There's no escaping the fact that believers need each other. We grow spiritually through ongoing interaction with persons who share our faith. This dependence is revealed in Solomon's emphasis on a teachable spirit in relationships:

"Let the wise listen and add to their learning, and let the discerning get guidance" (1:5).
"Instruct a wise man and he will be wiser" (9:9).
"The way of a fool seems right to him, but a wise man listens to advice" (12:15).
"As iron sharpens iron, so one man sharpens another" (27:17).

The need for teachers, counselors, and "sharpeners" doesn't give us the option of taking a Lone Ranger approach to following Christ. Here's how one philosopher summarized Proverbs' first insight: "He who will learn only from himself has a fool for a teacher."

Proverbs devotes a whopping amount of space to instructions on receiving criticism. At least nineteen different verses call for a teachable spirit in response to a critic's words. Here's a sampling:

"Rebuke a wise man and he will love you" (9:8).
"Whoever loves discipline loves knowledge, but he who hates correction is *stupid*" (12:1).
"He who ignores discipline comes to poverty and shame, but whoever heeds correction is honored" (13:18).
"He who listens to a life-giving rebuke will be at home among the wise. He who ignores discipline despises himself, but whoever heeds correction gains understanding" (15:31-32).
"A rebuke impresses a man of discernment more than a hundred lashes a fool" (17:10).
"A man who remains stiff-necked after many rebukes will suddenly be destroyed—without remedy" (29:1).

Critics aren't on target every time. And they don't always come across like honor graduates from the school of social etiquette. Yet Proverbs still holds us accountable for how we respond to them. Instead of muttering "Pardon me for living!" we're told to listen to them. Look at the following potentially positive results of a listening stance.

Whoever is willing to learn from a critic:

● *discovers the "way to life"* (6:23);
● *gets wiser* (9:9; 15:31; 19:20; 29:15);
● *will be honored* (13:18);
● *may enjoy a better-than-ever relationship with the critic* (9:8; 28:23).

The other side of the coin also deserves inspection. Proverbs discloses the negative consequences of a defensive, closed-minded response to critics.

Whoever is unwilling to learn from a critic:
- *"comes to poverty and shame"* (13:18);
- *receives stern discipline and physical or spiritual death* (15:10);
- *"will be destroyed without remedy"* (29:1);
- *hurts other people, such as his parents* (29:15).

Responding negatively to criticism also *increases our susceptibility to sin.* In Proverbs 5:1-14, Solomon warns us to avoid sex outside marriage. He knew from firsthand experience that loose morals lead to regret. Such a person will eventually cry, "How I hated discipline! How my heart spurned correction! I would not obey my teachers or listen to my instructors" (5:12-13). Solomon implies that an openness to caring critics early in life can prevent moral erosion. "He who forsakes reproof goes astray" (10:17, NASB).

In a mince-no-words style, God also labels people who don't cultivate a teachable spirit in response to criticism. He calls them "stupid" (12:1), "foolish" (10:8; 17:10), and "mockers" (9:8; 13:1).

Proverbs also offers some comments on *giving* criticism. The book implies that caring for others sometimes takes the form of confronting them. How they respond to us is an indication of *their* character. Whether we confront, and how we do it, is a reflection of *ours.* Consider these verses:

"Do not rebuke a mocker or he will hate you; rebuke a wise man and he will love you" (9:8).
"Better is open rebuke than hidden love. The kisses of an enemy may be profuse, but faithful are the wounds of a friend" (27:5-6).
"He who rebukes a man will in the end gain

more favor than he who has a flattering tongue"
(28:23).

Of course, not everyone responds to correction
with the spirit Eddie demonstrated in the opening
illustration. You've discovered that the long-term effect of a confrontation may be a closer relationship.
But just the opposite could occur. Even if we're tactful, people who are immature or insecure may resent
our confrontation and insult us (9:7-8). A few people
whose behavior warrants our criticism will use ear-
plugs when we speak (13:1). Others will avoid you if
you are willing to shoot straight with the truth. "A
mocker resents correction; he will not go to the
wise" (15:12).

As you read the following tips on receiving and giving criticism, think of actual encounters you've had that
can serve as reference points for self-evaluation.

Responsible Responses

When a teacher, coach, parent, or friend criticizes
you, it's like sitting on a tack: if the point is on target,
you're bound to feel pain. The next time someone
musters enough courage to confront you, respond in
a Proverbs-like manner by applying the following
tips. A few of these ideas I've learned in the classroom of experience. Others I've adapted from a booklet titled, *Practical Criticism: Giving It and Taking It*
(InterVarsity Press), by John Alexander.

● *Pray.* Ask the Lord to cultivate within you a
teachable rather than a *defensive* spirit. Ask for the
discernment to determine what's accurate, and
what's exaggerated, in the critic's observations. One
of the dog-eared pages in my copy of Gordon Mac-
Donald's *Ordering Your Private World* (Oliver-Nelson) offers this challenging anecdote:

HOW TO HANDLE A CRITIC

Dawson Trotman, the founder of the Navigators, had a good method for handling all criticisms directed at himself. No matter how unfair the criticism might seem to be, he would always take it into his prayer closet and in effect spread it before the Lord. Then he would say, "Lord, please show me the kernel of truth hidden in this criticism."

● *Let the critic finish.* Even if you think his or her opinion is wacky, resist the urge to interrupt. When our egos are threatened, snapping back is an almost automatic response. Remember Proverbs 29:11. "A fool gives full vent to his anger, but a wise man keeps himself under control." Before you respond to a critic, ask, "Is there anything else?" Also, let the person know you're listening by maintaining good eye contact with him.

● *To insure that you understand, restate or paraphrase the critic's observations.* Say something like, "I want to make sure I'm hearing you right. You are saying that . . . "

Sometimes we defend ourselves against charges that were never made. Checking for understanding can also keep you from exaggerating the situation. If a person says you were thoughtless on one occasion, he isn't necessarily labeling you an insensitive dolt.

● *If an apology is in order, be man or woman enough to do it quickly.* Putting it off only makes it harder to say you're sorry. Remember that *truth doesn't hurt— unless it ought to!* Also realize that it's difficult for most people to confront others. Set your critic at ease by thanking him or her for caring enough to approach you.

● *If you aren't immediately convinced the critic is correct, give yourself time to mull things over with a standard reply such as, "You could be right. I'll think*

about what you said." By saying this, you aren't con-
ceding anything. Yet you are telling the critic that
you're taking his or her input seriously. Such a response also keeps you from rash or thoughtless reaction. "Do you see a man who speaks in haste? There
is more hope for a fool than for him" (29:20). Thinking about a criticism gives you time to simmer down
and evaluate it more objectively.

● *To help you weigh the accuracy of a criticism follow
these steps:* (1) **Consider the source.** Ponder such
questions as, "Is the critic a person of integrity?"
"Does he or she have a history of loyalty to me?" "Is
the person gaining anything by knocking me, or is he
or she genuinely concerned about me or somebody
else I've hurt?" The more respect you have for the
person, the more likely he or she is on target with
the criticism. (2) **Consider the number of people
who have offered the same criticism.** When two
or more people volunteer the same painful observation, chances are their comments should be heeded.
(3) **Talk to a friend or adult whose opinion you
respect, and who knows you well.** Tell this person
what the critic said. Then ask: "Do you have the same
impression? Has this critic exposed something I need
to work on? How should I respond to him or her?"

Think of the last time you were on the receiving
end of what you'd call a rebuke. When you first heard
the other person's remarks, how did you feel? What
did you say or do in response to the criticism? Did
you later take the matter to the Lord and ask Him to
show you if the criticism was just? In view of the
previous suggestions for responding to a critic, what
would you change about your original reaction to the
incident? Applying these response tips to a past incident is a way of preparing for the next time it
happens.

HOW TO HANDLE A CRITIC

Caring Enough to Confront

Criticism is one thing which *isn't* always more blessed to give than to receive. Yet rebukes are often God's way of communicating His truth to people. Though we should proceed with caution, pointing out someone's weakness or mistake is often the right and loving thing to do. Gentle criticism is one of the things Solomon had in mind when he wrote, "The tongue of the wise brings healing" (12:18). Especially where sin is involved in the life of a Christian we know, it's our business to intervene. "If a man should be detected in some sin," wrote Paul, "the spiritual ones among you should quietly set him back on the right path, not with any feeling of superiority but being yourselves on guard against temptation" (Galatians 6:1, PH). Even when outright sin isn't involved, our words can still prod others to be and to do their best. "Let us consider how we may spur one another on toward love and good deeds" (Hebrews 10:24). Consider the following rules for giving *constructive* negative criticism.

• *Criticize the other person in private.* Your opinion will carry more weight if it isn't blurted out over the school's public address system. The easiest thing to do is vent your negative opinions behind the other person's back. But the *Christian* thing to do is to zip your lips until you speak directly to the individual. Jesus said, "If your brother wrongs you, go and have it out with him at once—*just between the two of you*" (Matthew 18:15, PH, emphasis mine).

• *When possible, write out what you plan to say.* Writing an imaginary conversation in your diary or journal can help you sort through the issue, and assign correct labels to your feelings. When the uncomfortable moment of confrontation arrives, you're less likely to grope for words or chicken out. And you're more apt to speak in a sensitive tone of voice.

WISE UP

Sometimes it's OK to put your criticism in the form of a letter. (That's how Sandy reacted to Eddie's unfair remarks about Andrea in the opening illustration.) If you're pretty sure your courage will evaporate when you're eyeball-to-eyeball with the person, or if you think the individual's defensiveness won't give you a chance to finish, jot down your feelings instead. Close the note, though, with an offer to talk things over later. Whether you write a note or verbalize your feelings, the Lord can guide you in your choice of words. "For the Lord gives wisdom, and from His mouth come knowledge and understanding" (Proverbs 2:6).

Back in high school, I had a crush on a cheerleader named Mary. Between classes, I tagged along behind her up and down the halls. I told friends how I felt about her. I stuffed mushy poems in her locker. Yet I was so shy that I went over a year without speaking to her face-to-face. I'm sure that my eerie behavior aggravated Mary. And my reputation as a charter member of the school's "Nerd Club" didn't enhance her opinion of me either. She had every right to hire an assassin to take care of me. Instead she gave me a dose of my own medicine and wrote me the following poem:

NOW YOU KNOW

I wish there was some way you could know
Without my having to tell you so.
It makes me feel good when things you say,
Are aimed at me, directed my way.

I know you're sweet, kind and true.
The world needs more guys like you.
But all in all, when this thing ends,
I'd just rather we'd be friends.

Mary's rejection of my romantic interest hurt, all right. Yet she chose a sensitive way to criticize my peculiar behavior. Her tact definitely softened the blow.

• *Make sure you've earned the right to be heard.* How long have you known the other person? Do you have a track record of loyalty to him or her? According to Proverbs, unsolicited advice is more apt to be heeded in a warm relational climate. "Faithful are the wounds of a friend" (27:6). Painful words are more welcome when they're delivered by someone who cares.

• *Don't jump to conclusions about the person's motives.* Speculating about motives fogs the real issue. Keep the focus on observable behavior or attitudes. Which would you rather hear—"I feel irritated when you keep me waiting for so long" or "You're not fooling anybody, you're just trying to get me mad by showing up late"?

• *Qualify your remarks.* Avoid words like "never" and "always." Put the spotlight on a specific mistake or trait. If a friend acts insensitively once, don't imply that he makes the same mistake day-in and day-out.

• *Ask questions in a tactful way to launch a confrontation.* Questions give the recipient the benefit of the doubt and allow him to explain his motives. This procedure insures that you have sufficient evidence on which to base critical remarks you have planned. Asking questions is a practical way to avoid the speech snare referred to in Proverbs 29:20. "Do you see a man who speaks in haste? There is more hope for a fool than for him." Which is better: "What you said about Becky was terrible! You must be jealous of her!" or "Why did you say those things about Becky?"

As we close this chapter, let's keep two things in mind. First, when it comes to *receiving* criticism, remember that good advice is worthless *unless you follow it.* And second, when it comes to *giving* criticism, be sure your reason for confronting is an unselfish one.

8
BANK ON IT!

The following true story is dedicated to cooks of all ages who enjoy the challenge of preparing an "original" dish.

A friend of mine ate dog food one evening. No, he wasn't at a fraternity initiation or a hobo party . . . he was actually at an elegant student reception in a physician's home near Miami. The dog food was served on delicate little crackers with a wedge of imported cheese, bacon chips, an olive, and a sliver of pimento on top. That's right, friends and neighbors, it was hors d'oeuvres à la Alpo.

The hostess is a first-class nut! You gotta know her to appreciate the story. She had just graduated from a gourmet cooking course, and so she decided it was time to put her skill to the ultimate test. Did she ever! After doctoring up those miserable morsels and putting them on a couple of silver trays, with a sly grin she watched them disappear. One guy (my friend) couldn't get enough. He kept coming back for more. I don't recall how they broke the news to him . . . but when he found out the truth, he probably barked and bit her on the leg! He certainly must have gagged a little (Charles Swindoll, *Growing Strong in the Seasons of Life,* Multnomah).

What a perfect illustration of *deception!* The hostess tricked her guests into thinking they were eating expensive snack food concocted in her upper-class kitchen. Instead, she made her pet cocker spaniel howling mad by robbing him of his supper. After telling this story, Swindoll goes on to discuss the fine art of deception:

If you want to make a counterfeit dollar bill, you don't use yellow construction paper, cut it in the shape of triangle, put the Lone Ranger's picture in the center, and stamp "3" on each corner. That deceives nobody. Deception comes in a *convincing* fashion, wearing the garb of authenticity, supported by the credentials of intelligence, popularity, and even a touch of class. By the millions, gullible gluttons are duped into swallowing lies, thinking all the while they are digesting the truth. In reality they are underscoring the well-worn words of Phineas Taylor Barnum: *"There's a sucker born every minute"* (*Growing Strong in the Seasons of Life*).

This is the first of two chapters which discuss one of the most delicious deceptions ever served up by Satan. He expertly disguises the truth and serves this delectable morsel to millions of people: *The key to happiness is "having."* Satan says that *the more money and material things we accumulate, the more meaningful our lives will be.* At first what he offers satisfies the tastebuds. The more we digest his philosophy, though, the sicker we get. Anyone who keeps picking from Satan's platter eventually gags on the contents. After all, no matter how you decorate it, Alpo is *still* dog food!

You'll discover that Proverbs doesn't necessarily condemn you for buying a new stereo or sports car. No one gets spiritual brownie points just because he's poor. In fact, Proverbs applauds diligence on the job and salutes people who get wealthy because they work hard. But the Book of Proverbs does expose the foolishness of placing too much emphasis on riches and working solely for selfish reasons. And it suggests that a passion for material things siphons off our devotion to God and hinders our usefulness to Him.

Earthly Minded

Before we delve into Proverbs, let's take a look at some trends concerning spending habits and attitudes toward money—particularly, the trends of people in your age group.

● A recent survey of more than 200,000 entering freshmen at 590 colleges indicated a growing trend toward materialism. Of the people surveyed, 76 percent listed financial prosperity as an "essential" or "very important" life goal. Yet only 39 percent of the same group listed "developing a meaningful philosophy of life" as important. That's in stark contrast to a similar survey of college freshmen taken twenty years ago. At that time, 83 percent listed "a meaningful philosophy of life" as a key goal. Alexander Astin, director of the more recent survey, concludes, "Our data show that greed is alive and well!" He says the trend toward materialism has been rising steadily in recent years. "Obviously we're seeing something very profound in society," he admits (*New York Times,* 14 January 1988).

● A group called Empty Tomb, Inc. studied the giving patterns in 31 Christian denominations. Although average income after taxes rose 31 percent between 1968 and 1985, per-member church giving dropped almost 9 percent. Though this survey included church giving by all ages of people, young people are definitely following the pattern of progressive stinginess. According to Tom Sine, in his book *Why Settle for More and Miss the Best?* (Word), Christians under the age of 35 give significantly less to Christian organizations than do those over 35 — despite evidence that the young are better off than they've ever been. "As this younger population ages," writes Sine, "the economic base of all kinds of Christian enterprises will be in trouble if we don't teach our young people to look beyond themselves" (as reported in *Youthworker Update,* April 1989).

● A growing educational trend is to introduce high school students to the outside world by having them set up real companies — organizations run with *real* money, not Monopoly money. "The idea is to let kids know that they have a role in the local market place," says Robert Reinke, who monitors trends in the New York school curriculum. But some experts worry that these programs increase teens' attraction to materialistic values. According to *Wall Street Journal* writer Alex Freidman, reporting on a gathering of teen entrepreneurs at the University of Pennsylvania's Wharton School, "These teens crave excitement. They dream about power and pots of money. Especially money."

One teen jewelry importer told him, "There's never too much money. I want enough money to go anywhere, anytime, at a moment's notice, by any means." Another teen who runs a computer business in Florida reported, "If you've worked hard for your money—and this will sound greedy—it's yours. There should be no pressure or obligation to give any of it up" (*Youthworker Update*, February 1987).

• In 1988, teens spent over $55 billion! That figure was up $1.3 billion from 1987. According to the Rand Youth Poll, with the teen population having peaked back in 1975, "20% *fewer* people are now spending 117% *more* money." More teens are working for pay too. *Seventeen* magazine reports that the annual income of the average 13–19-year-old girl is $2,902, of which she spends all but $422 (*Youthworker Update*, April 1989).

Where do *you* fit into these statistics and trends? At some point those teen tycoons—and all who share their sentiments—will discover what King Solomon learned the hard way: *The less you have to live for, the more you need to live on.*

True Riches

Seven words capture the main point Proverbs makes on the subject of material resources: *Money has never yet made anyone rich*—at least, not in God's economy. People who live for their bank accounts and allow *things* to replace God's Son in their lives miss out on more valuable assets. Solomon, who lived to regret a self-indulgent lifestyle, finally admitted that *"The blessing of the Lord* brings wealth" (Proverbs 10:22, emphasis mine). And he wasn't referring to material blessings.

Why does the Bible frequently warn us about the magnetic pull of a "more" mentality? Because material investments pale in comparison to the worth of spiritual stock. The following are some of the things God puts a higher price tag on than a $100 monthly allowance and a closet full of designer labels.

- *A good name.* "A good name is more desirable than great riches; to be esteemed is better than silver or gold" (22:1). This isn't a reference to popularity. It's talking about the rare and precious commodity of Christian character. When people see or hear your name, what pops into their minds? Is your name synonymous with integrity?

- *Wisdom.* "Blessed is the man who finds wisdom . . . for she is more profitable than silver and yields better returns than gold" (3:13-14). In Proverbs 8:11 Solomon adds, "Wisdom is more precious than rubies, and nothing you desire can compare with her." He was referring to the kind of discernment and common sense that comes only from God. "The fear of the Lord is the beginning of wisdom, and knowledge of the Holy One is understanding (9:10). Remember these words: "The Lord gives wisdom, and from His mouth come knowledge and understanding. He holds victory in store for the upright" (2:6-7).

- *Truthfulness.* Most people get their cash the old-fashioned way: they *earn* it! But compromising integrity in order to make a buck is still more common than Lincoln pennies. God says it is "better to be poor than a liar" (19:22). Besides, spending money obtained dishonestly will haunt people in the long run. "A fortune made by a lying tongue is a fleeting vapor and a deadly snare" (21:6). If God doesn't mete out their punishment in the here and now, frauds will get their just due when Jesus returns to earth. "Wealth is worthless in the day of wrath, but righteousness delivers from death" (11:4).

● *Lips of knowledge.* Teaching others—especially when it comes to sharing God's truth—is a wiser investment than emeralds. "There is gold, and an abundance of jewels; but the lips of knowledge are a more precious thing" (20:15, NASB). Whenever the glitter of a gemstone tantalizes my eyes, that verse puts my Bible teacher's salary in proper perspective.

● *Harmonious relationships.* "Better is a little with the fear of the Lord than great wealth with turmoil. Better a meal of vegetables where there is love than a fattened calf with hatred" (15:16-17). I don't know about you, but I'd rather eke out a living than go bankrupt in my relationships. Who can put a price tag on the gift of other people's love, or on a sense of belonging to somebody else?

Waist-ed Gold

None of the verses you've read in this chapter condemn money. God merely wants us to see its relative importance in comparison to other treasures. So long as they don't possess us, possessions aren't a problem. God's warning is reserved for people who worship at the altar of wealth, who bracket off the financial area of their lives from divine influence. "Whoever trusts in his riches will fall" (11:28).

Yussif, a professional wrestler nicknamed the "Terrible Turk," needed that reminder two generations ago. He literally demonstrated the truth of Proverbs 11:28. The 350-pound behemoth grabbed athletic glory all over Europe and the United States. In a match against the United States' best wrestler, Yussif tossed the American champ across the ring like a teddy bear, then pinned him. The Terrible

Turk demanded the $5,000 winner's purse in gold coins. When he boarded the ship back to Europe, he crammed the gold coins into his huge belt. During the voyage, the ship began to sink. The wrestler went over the side with his bulging belt full of gold still strapped to his enormous waist. The added weight kept him from staying afloat until the lifeboats could arrive. Yussif and his gold plunged straight to the bottom of the Atlantic. Neither before nor since that day has the value of gold ever sunk so fast! (Charles Swindoll, *Growing Strong in the Seasons of Life*)

If God leads you to pursue a degree in business or plops you into a job that earns six figures, you don't owe anyone an apology—not as long as you keep material things in proper perspective, and make it a habit to invest in those less tangible commodities deemed more precious by God.

9

RELEASING
YOUR RESOURCES

The *Oakland Tribune* recently ran a "How Cheap Are You?" contest. The newspaper asked readers to submit their money-saving ideas. The responses revealed skinflints in the categories of gross, tacky, unbelievable, incredible, and downright dishonest.

A retired welder won top tightwad honors. To save coins, he separates two-ply toilet paper. Among the gross, a Berkeley couple said they save dental floss on a bathroom hook so it can be reused. Another reader claims he refreezes used ice cubes.

As for tacky, one couple collects two-for-one coupons to restaurants, then invites another couple. "We make them pay for their half, and we dine free," they reported. In the unbelievable category, another reader wrote, "I regulate my bodily functions so that I go to the bathroom only during working hours. It saves on water, tissue, and time at home. I can spend my hours at home doing something constructive, like cutting off expiration dates on coupons."

An incredible submission came from a man in El Cerrito. When his vacuum cleaner bag fills, he cuts one end, empties it, and sews it up for reuse. "Not only does it save bags, but sometimes I find a penny in the dust," he asserted. Another man keeps a paper bag in his car with "Out of Order" printed on it. He places the bag on parking meters next to his car! (From an Associated Press article, "Economy Is One Thing, But . . . " *The State* newspaper, Columbia, S.C., 22 February 1989.)

Save all the coupons, ice cubes, and dental floss you want. God doesn't mind. But He *doesn't* want such a miserly attitude seeping into your relationship with Him or other people.

Gaining through Giving
The Book of Proverbs unveils an unmistakable insight: *One reason God endows us with money-making ability is to give us a means of helping less fortunate people.*

How we treat the poor of this world is a barometer of our affection for God. Note how the Lord identifies with the needy:

> "He who mocks the poor shows contempt for their Maker" (17:5).
> "He who oppresses the poor shows contempt for their Maker, but whoever is kind to the needy honors God" (14:31).
> "He who is kind to the poor lends to the Lord" (19:17).

Jesus further emphasized divine identification with the poor. After encouraging His followers to feed the hungry, clothe the naked, and visit the sick and imprisoned, He said, "Whatever you did for one of the least of these brothers of mine, you did for me" (Matthew 25:40).

Various passages in Proverbs also reveal the benefits of an *open handed,* as opposed to a *tight fisted,* policy. When we share with others instead of squirreling away things solely for our own consumption, look what we have to gain:

"A generous man will prosper" (Proverbs 11:25).
"He who gives to the poor will lack nothing, but he who closes his eyes to them receives many curses" (28:27).
"A generous man will himself be blessed, for he shares his food with the poor" (22:9).
"Blessed is he who is kind to the needy" (14:21).

God isn't guaranteeing you a beachfront condo or early retirement if you help poor people. But he does say He'll take care of unselfish people. And ironically, He insists that the gratification of giving beats the giddiness of receiving anytime. The equation of joy and giving sometimes seems foreign to some of us. But check it out. Few penny-pinchers stay happy for very long. I read about a billionaire oil magnate who couldn't enjoy his wealth. He was so uptight about losing it that he installed a pay phone in his mansion for overnight guests. To top it all off, he saved on electricity by replacing all 100-watt light bulbs in his house with the 60-watt variety. He died wealthier, all right. And miserable.

WISE UP

We can't separate Christianity and meeting needs of hurting people. Verses like Proverbs 29:7 won't let us. "The righteous care about justice for the poor, but the wicked have no such concern."

Your involvement with poverty, whether in your hometown or overseas, can take many forms. You can donate clothes that you've outgrown to the Salvation Army or some other local relief agency. Why clutter your closet in anticipation of a garage sale when scores of families in your area can't even afford a trip to K-Mart? You can take a summer missions trip to a poverty-stricken part of the world. If nothing else, the exposure will prove that you're materially better off than you think. It's eye-opening to compare yourself with people in the rest of the world instead of with your classmates who live in an adjacent subdivision. (For information on such a venture, chat with your church's youth director or write Teen Missions International, 885 Hall Rd., Merritt Island, FL 32953.)

Numerous Christian agencies exist to help channel funds and supplies to needy people all over the world. One of the best known is World Vision, a nonprofit agency that provides emergency aid, furthers evangelism, and increases public awareness of poverty around the globe. Drop them a line. (You can write them at World Vision, 919 W. Huntington Dr., Monrovia, CA 91016.) Ask them to increase your awareness of the needs of the poor and to inform you of realistic ways you can pitch in and help. You won't have to wait long for a reply.

We've heard all our lives that it's better to give than to receive. Yet it's clear that most of us are willing to let the other fellow have the blessing! Perhaps the following poem will jar our thinking and spur us to action:

I was hungry
And you formed a humanities club
And discussed my hunger.
Thank you.
I was in prison
and you crept off quietly
and prayed for my release.
I was naked
and in your mind you debated
the morality of my appearance.
I was sick
and you knelt
and thanked God for your health.
I was lonely
and you left me alone to pray for me.
You seem so holy,
So close to God, but
I'm still very hungry and lonely and cold.
So where have your prayers gone?
What does it profit a man
To page through his book of prayers
When the rest of the world is
Crying for his help?

(Taken from "Rich Religion: The Hundredfold Heresy," by Danny Lehmann, a brochure from Last Days Ministries.)

At least now you have an idea of what to do with all the money you save on two-ply toilet paper, used dental floss, leftover ice cubes, and surgically repaired vacuum-cleaner bags.

God as Your Banker

Chuck Swindoll writes more books in a year than some people read in a lifetime. In a hefty hardback titled *Living Above the Level of Mediocrity* (Word) he tells a sobering story:

I have a close friend in the ministry who traveled across the country for a week of meetings. The only problem was, his baggage didn't make it. As I recall, the bags went to Berlin! He really needed a couple of suits. So he went down to the local thrift shop and was pleased to find a row of suits. When he told the guy, "I'd like to get a couple of suits," the salesman said, "Good, we've got several. But you need to know that they came from the local mortuary. They've all been cleaned and pressed, but they were used on stiffs. Not a thing wrong with them, I just didn't want that to bother you." My friend said, "No, that's fine. That's okay." So he hurriedly tried some on and bought a couple for about twenty-five bucks apiece. Great deal!

When he got back to his room, he began to get dressed for the evening's meeting. As he put one on, to his surprise there were no pockets. Both sides were all sewed up! Though surprised, he thought, "Why of course! Stiffs don't carry stuff with 'em when they depart!" The suits looked as if they had pockets, but they were just flaps on the coat. My friend told me later, "I spent all week trying to stick my hands in my pockets. Wound up having to hang my keys on my belt!" The minister was reminded all week long that life is temporal.

That anecdote illustrates another major observation about money offered by Proverbs: *When evaluated from an eternal perspective, making material wealth our main objective in life is foolish; only the resources we invest in God's work reap guaranteed dividends.*

Our years on earth don't represent one-billionth of our existence. If God's Word makes anything clear, it's the fact that life doesn't end with death. How tragic it is to say we *believe* in eternity, but spend our lives as if it were a myth.

The fact that this realm of time and space is temporary, yet human life goes on forever, sheds new light on Proverbs 28:19. "He who follows empty pursuits will have poverty in plenty" (NASB). God is saying that the rich man who neglects the spiritual dimension is bankrupt when it comes to lasting values. Possessions in the here and now cannot influence our eternal destinies, for "riches do not endure forever" (27:24). When this phase of our existence comes to a screeching halt—either at death or Christ's return—*everybody's* bank accounts go back to zero. Perhaps that's what Solomon had in mind when he wrote, "Do not wear yourself out to get rich; have the wisdom to show restraint. Cast but a glance at riches, and they are gone, for they will surely sprout wings and fly off to the sky like an eagle" (23:4-5).

The New Testament echoes Proverbs' warning about preoccupation with the temporary. Jesus had some hard words for people who are too earthly minded to be of any heavenly good. He said, "Do not store up for yourselves treasures on earth, where moth and rust destroy, and where thieves break in and steal. But store up for yourselves treasures in heaven, where moth and rust do not destroy, and where thieves do not break in and steal. For where your treasure is, there your heart will be also" (Matthew 6:19-21). Anyone who has the kind of heavenly heart Jesus talked about takes Proverbs 3:9 seriously. "Honor the Lord with your wealth." That's simply another way of saying, "Don't spend all your money on yourself. Invest part of it to spread the Christian message and support the work of God throughout the world."

Monumental Decisions

My main fear in discussing this eternal versus temporal investment issue is that you'll get the wrong impression. Whoever believes the Bible outlaws savings
accounts and mutual funds is going off the deep end.
Yet it *is* essential to keep the communication lines
with God open and allow the Holy Spirit to ask us
hard questions about our resources—financial and
otherwise.

● Is our basic orientation in life aimed at material
pursuits, or at permanent commodities such as a relationship with Christ and His work in the world?

● Are we demonstrating our love for the Lord by
giving a portion of our income to His work in the
local church?

● Are we using our time, energies, and talents for
the Lord in any way? Or does the job we took to pay
off a car loan leave us too exhausted to get involved
at church, or with other Christian organizations?

● Do we exercise concern for the eternal destiny of
family members and friends by praying for their salvation? By sharing Christ with them?

● Could we mow lawns, or work a few extra hours
at Arby's, to help support a summer missions trip
planned by a peer in the youth group?

Whenever the Holy Spirit questioned R.G.
LeTourneau about stewardship of his resources,
LeTourneau listened intently. He started out as an
engineer during the Depression of the 1930s. From
the start, he decided to use money to build God's
kingdom, not just his own business. By the time he
died decades later, he had gone from living on 90
percent of his income and giving away 10 percent to
just the opposite. He kept 10 percent and gave 90
percent to churches and missions groups!
LeTourneau felt that such a financial move was logi-

cal in view of the Christian message about heaven and hell. He wanted as many people as possible to hear the Gospel. LeTourneau realized that the hearse which would carry his body to the cemetery *wouldn't have a luggage rack!*

His example is in sharp contrast to another man I heard about. Let's pick up the other fellow's story in a book I wrote a few years ago:

Go to a graveyard outside Lincoln, Kansas, and you'll see an unusual group of gravestones. They were erected by a man named Davis. When you delve into his personal history, you discover that he began working as a lowly hired hand. Over the years, though, by sheer determination and extreme frugality, he amassed a wallet-bulging fortune. You also find out that Mr. Davis's preoccupation with wealth resulted in a neglect of people. Apparently he had few friends. He was even emotionally distant from his wife's family, who felt that she had married beneath her dignity. Their attitude embittered him. He vowed never to leave his relatives a penny.

When his wife died, Davis hired a sculptor to design an elaborate monument in her memory. The monument consisted of a love seat showing Mr. Davis and his wife sitting together. The result so pleased him that he paid for another showing him kneeling at his wife's grave, placing a wreath on it. That was followed by a third monument — showing his wife kneeling at his future gravesite. His monument-building binge continued until he'd spent more than a quarter of a million dollars!

He was often approached about contributing

financial aid to worthwhile projects in the town or church. But he rarely gave to them. Most of his small fortune was invested in gravestones. At 92, Mr. Davis died—a sour-hearted resident of the poorhouse.

Decades later, as you saunter through the graveyard, you notice an ironic fact: each monument he commissioned is slowly sinking into the Kansas soil, a victim of neglect, vandalism, and time. Inevitably, these temporal objects will follow him into the grave.

We're instinctively repelled by such an eccentric expenditure of time and money. "What a waste!" we're prone to cry. We think of loftier, less selfish pursuits that could have enhanced the lives of countless people.

Yet Mr. Davis' strange investments may still reap dividends—if we let the story of his life serve as a stimulus for evaluating our own lives. When is the last time you evaluated how you are investing your life? Consider these soul-jarring questions:

● What are God's objectives for my life?

● To what extent am I investing my life and God-given resources in eternal, rather than just temporal, matters?

● What "monuments" do I want to leave behind when I die? (*Welcome to Your Ministry*, David C. Cook)

Ask God to be your broker. Give Him permission to evaluate your "investment portfolio" and make any necessary changes.

10

LET'S HEAR IT
FOR MOM!

A few years ago I spotted an unusual headline in my daily newspaper: "Macho Ex-Marine Admits Failure As 'Housewife'"

The United Press International feature described the sobering experience of Bob Peters, a former marine and Stanford All-American defensive end who can bench press 400 pounds. For nine months of the year, the former Palo Alto Jaycee Man of the Year is a high school football and wrestling coach. When June rolled around, his wife took a summer job while he stayed home with their four kids, ages four to sixteen. He signed a 70-day "Motherhood" contract which spelled out his responsibilities: tutor, financial manager, arbitrator, disciplinarian, chef, recreational director, and maid, to name a few.

How did he fare? "It's an impossible task for any human being," he concluded. "I really didn't realize it was so hard. I'm in good physical condition. I'm big and strong, but since I've been doing this, I've lost 10 pounds that I didn't want to lose. It's because of the running around, getting up early and staying up late."

Peters says he didn't come close to achieving all the goals in the contract, but at least he learned the hard way that "a mom's job is not one of viewing one soap opera after another and hosting Tupperware parties and such." Peters says the President should appoint a national commission "to promote a renaissance of respect and admiration for mothers everywhere."

Peters' experiment shows that if motherhood isn't the toughest job in the world, it ranks right up there with fighting forest fires or serving as an arbitrator for a Middle East conflict. Centuries before anyone officially stamped "Mother's Day" on the calendar, the Lord honored wives and mothers in a 22-verse salute at the end of Proverbs. Traditionally, Proverbs 31:10-31 has been tabbed a "mirror for a godly woman." Females can look at this portrait and identify qualities that God wants to cultivate in their character. But there's another way to view the passage. You can regard it as a handbook on the worth of a wife or mother. The passage discusses various dimensions of the woman's role, covering everything from her muscle-stretching chores to her spiritual influence. Before we delve into the passage, take a minute to read Proverbs 31:10-31 in your Bible.

If you're like me, you concluded that this exalted portrait of a wife and mother belongs in an art gallery, not in a house. "Who measures up to this ideal?" you may be thinking. "Besides, aren't the duties listed in the passage a bit prehistoric? How many moms in this day and age make jeans and sweaters for their kids? In an era when most moms work outside the home, how many of them crawl out of bed before sunrise to cook French toast and sausage? Frosted Flakes or Egg McMuffins are the rule, not the exception."

If you're asking those questions, I commend you. The questions indicate that you're interacting with the material. But whether or not today's woman performs all the tasks mentioned in Proverbs 31 isn't the point. Don't think the Bible is a straitjacket condemning the female to a rigid, suffocating routine. What we're after are the character traits reflected in the household responsibilities outlined in the passage. By itemizing the types of contributions made by this ideal woman, we'll discover the value of the more down-to-earth women in *our* lives.

May the following pages increase your appreciation for the lady of *your* house.

Wonder Woman

The lady depicted in Proverbs 31 didn't need a Jane Fonda workout video to help her get in shape. Her house was one big exercise spa! Think of the calories she burned in the following activities from her schedule:

"She selects wool and flax
and works with eager hands.
She is like the merchant ships,
bringing her food from afar.
She gets up while it is still dark;
she provides food for her family and portions for her servant girls.
She considers a field and buys it;
out of her earnings she plants a vineyard" (vv. 13-16).

"In her hands she holds the distaff
and grasps the spindle with her fingers" (v. 19).
"She makes coverings for her bed" (v. 22).
"She makes linen garments and sells them,
and supplies the merchants with sashes" (v. 24).
"She watches over the affairs of her household
and does not eat the bread of idleness" (v. 27).

Shopping, cooking, sewing, gardening—it's no wonder verse 17 says "her arms are strong for her tasks." In the days before automobiles, microwaves, washers and dryers, and garden tillers, her routine made her the arm-wrestling champ of the family! On top of it all, the woman pictured here earned a part-time income. Maybe that's why she hired maids to help with the housework (v. 15).

Perk up your ears, and you may hear God's Spirit whisper the following questions: *What taken-for-granted physical chores does your mom perform on a regular basis? How does the diligence modeled by the Proverbs 31 woman show up in her?* Even if you're from a home where Dad and the kids pitch in around the house, chances are Mom works overtime to meet your basic needs. (Remember Bob Peters? He'd say "Amen" to that remark!)

In *Heroes And Zeroes* (SonPower), I used the following illustration to show how easy it is to take moms for granted:

> While I was relaxing with the evening paper recently, the following headline grabbed my attention: "Striking Mother and Her Teenagers Near Agreement." The UPI story told of a working mom who went on strike against her three teenagers when they complained about housework left undone.

LET'S HEAR IT FOR MOM!

The mom worked as a waitress and part-time school bus driver. Yet the teens still expected her to do all the household chores. When one of them muttered, "Mom, you never do anything!" she officially launched her strike. She stopped cooking meals, washing clothes, vacuuming, and performing other mundane chores. As you can imagine, the mess piled up for the next week or two. She wrote work contracts for the children to sign and had these agreements notarized.

During week two of the strike, the teens gave in and cleaned up the house. But they still refused to sign the contracts. The mother compromised and began making their school lunches again. At the time the article was printed, both sides were hammering out compromises to the contracts. The mom told a reporter, "In the future, work around here will be split up real evenly on a rotating basis. I feel it was a learning experience for the kids and myself. I guess I had been a hindrance to them during growing up years by doing everything for them. And it showed them that they took for granted a lot of what I do as a mother."

To keep your mom from walking the picket line, mull over what you can do to lighten her load. Don't treat her like the teens in the previous story treated their mother. They saw their mom as another household appliance—noticing her only when she *didn't* work, then griping about it.

House Executive
One myth that needs to be dispelled is that a mother's contribution to the family is limited to physical

labor that any healthy person could perform. Proverbs 31 does not typecast Mom as some Snow White, who lives cheerfully in a forest of social isolation, dutifully cleaning the cottage as she waits for her man and the little dwarves to dribble home at the end of the day.

Proverbs' maternal portrait shows a person with a highly developed brain as well as steel-plated biceps. Her role requires managerial ability that would make any Fortune 500 company look twice at her resume. Taking care of a family is like running a small business. And in most homes, even where Dad is chairman of the board, most administrative duties are delegated to you-know-who.

Look closer at the Proverbs 31 portrait and you'll see the following evidences of managerial know-how:

● *Delegation.* The size of her house and family made it necessary to hire outside help. Her early-morning duties included planning the schedules of her employees. The "portions" given to her servant girls in verse 15 refers to prescribed tasks. To keep a work crew happy and productive takes more administrative genius than you think.

● *Money management.* She budgeted money for the food and fabric needed to sustain the family (vv. 13-14). With leftover fabric, she made garments to display at weekend garage sales (v. 24). That action required the expertise of an accountant: figuring out profit margins, sale prices, and so forth. She invested her earnings in real estate, purchasing a garden plot as a way to help satisfy the appetites of her family members (v. 16). Planning was an integral part of her agenda. She did an annual inventory of her kids' closets, anticipated their needs for winter wardrobes, then made the clothes they'd need months in advance (v. 21).

• *Wise counsel.* Proverbs 31 also applauds the wisdom of a woman's words. "She speaks with wisdom" (v. 26). With few exceptions, God has given women a special ability to think practically, and to employ wisdom in specific situations that come up. That wisdom enables women to make smart managerial decisions, and to offer sound advice when consulted about a problem.

A man asked his wife to help him pick out a new family car. As a salesman escorted them along a row of new models, the woman kept wanting to see the trunk of each car. After several trunk inspections, the frustrated salesman blurted, "Lady, most folks inspect the engine rather than the trunk!"

Her reply? "I assume that any engine will run OK for a few years. But you can't determine the size of the trunk without looking. We travel a lot, and luggage always ends up under our feet and behind our heads. So just keep opening the trunk, please."

On a scale of 1–10, how would you rank *your* mom's administrative skill? This passage in Proverbs is demonstrating that managing a household takes brains as well as brawn. Even moms who aren't executive material fulfill more managerial functions than we give them credit for. Keeping your closet stocked and food in the cupboard requires planning—"putting the future into the present tense."

Expanding Walls

The profile in Proverbs 31 indicates that a woman's *primary* responsibility is to her husband and kids. Yet you get the impression that the woman described here wasn't trapped within the four walls of her house. Her gifts and abilities weren't kept under lock and key. Far from being a social invalid, she supplemented her substantial commitment to the family with dimensions of fulfillment outside the house.

We've already discussed how she used her proficiency as a tailor to supplement her husband's income (v. 24). And we've seen how she invested her earnings as she saw fit (v. 16). But the scope of her influence widens even more in verse 20. "She opens her arms to the poor and extends her hands to the needy." One result of her efficient family management and relief work in the community was a lofty reputation for her husband. Her contributions increased the respect his peers had for him (v. 23). They realized how smart he was for marrying her!

If it weren't for the contributions of moms and housewives, the fabric of society would unravel. In what ways does your mom's scope of influence extend beyond the four walls of your house? Does she work for money in order to save for your college tuition? Does she teach a rowdy gang of kids week after week in Sunday School, or write letters of encouragement to hurting people? Does she cook for the neighbors when the lady of the house is ill? Does she visit people in the hospital? Chances are your mother is making many more contributions—in and out of the home—than you realize!

Spiritual Savvy

What motivates the Proverbs 31 woman to serve her family and community selflessly? *Her close bond with the Lord!* Her wisdom and diligence sprout from spiritual soil that's regularly cultivated.

According to verse 30, her most praiseworthy trait is a reverence for God. "Charm is deceptive, and beauty is fleeting; but a woman who fears the Lord is to be praised." More important than her social standing or appointments with her hairdresser is nurturing her relationship with the Lord. And her spiritual zeal is contagious.

John Wesley was the founder of the Methodist Church in the 18th century. His brother Charles wrote hundreds of Christian hymns, many of which are in the hymnals we use every Sunday. What accounted for their immeasurable contributions to church history? A devout mother. Susanna Wesley gave birth to seventeen kids, yet she locked herself in her room for one hour every day just to pray for them.

Maybe your mom doesn't reserve a prayer closet for sixty minutes a day, but odds are that her spiritual savvy improves the atmosphere in your home. What evidences of a heart for God do you see in her? How has she invested in *your* spiritual development? Have you ever thanked her for the prayers she's said on your behalf? If she isn't in close touch with God, how can you encourage her spiritual resurgence? If she isn't a Christian, do you pray regularly for her salvation? Prayer is an acceptable way to rebel against the status quo in any unbeliever's life.

If your mom does exert a positive spiritual influence, let Abraham Lincoln's words make a deep impression on you. "No person is poor who has a godly mother."

Monumental Praise

The person who painted this female portrait in Proverbs 31 put a clincher on it in verses 28-29. "Her children arise and call her blessed; her husband also, and he praises her: 'Many women do noble things, but you surpass them all.'" When it comes to gratitude, does your mom get the short end of the stick? Few people need voice lessons to sing their own praises, but to compliment the work and character of others is a different matter. The verses we read call for expressions of appreciation on our part.

WISE UP

The majestic Statue of Liberty towers above the entrance to New York Harbor, a symbol of the freedom we enjoy here in America. It was a gift to the United States from the French government. A famous sculptor named Bartholdi devoted twenty years to creating the statue, even investing most of his own fortune to help the French government meet expenses of the project. From the start, Bartholdi looked for a model whose form and features he could reproduce as "Lady Liberty." After examining a list of famous and heroic women, he selected the model: *his own mother!*

You, too, can raise a monument to your mom by finding creative ways to express your appreciation. A teen I know did a flip-flop in his attitude toward his mom when she was bedridden with an illness. He gave her the following poem:

Taken for Granted
Some moms get taken out to dinner
    at a restaurant fit for a queen.
Then they're taken where waists get thinner —
    to a spa that can make them lean.
Others get taken on a second honeymoon,
    or a cruise to a place enchanted.
But moms like you, more often than not,
    just get *taken for granted!*

If you aren't a poet, look for other ways to build a monument in your mother's honor. Does one of the following ideas grab you?

● *Empty Envelope.* Lick a stamp and put it in the corner of a letter envelope. Write your mom's name and address on the envelope. Go ahead and seal the envelope. (Yeah, I know it's empty. Just follow directions.) On the *back* of the envelope jot down these words: "Mom, inside this envelope you'll discover what my life would be like without you." Then mail it.

- *First-Class Gratitude.* This time put a letter in the envelope. Start the note with, "I thank God for you because _____." Think of specific ways to fill in the blank.

- *Sumptuous Spread.* Get your dad in on this one. Reserve a table at your mom's favorite restaurant. During the meal, each of you take turns telling one thing you appreciate about her. (One more thing— don't give her the check!)

- *Surprise Symbol.* Go to a Christian bookstore or a craft shop and pick out a wall plaque or other decorative item for the house. Pay for it with your own money. Tell your mom it's a concrete way of thanking her for her contributions to the family. Every time she sees it, she'll realize that her work isn't taken for granted.

Without draining your bank account or slicing twenty years off your life, *you* can build your own version of the Statue of Liberty in honor of *your* mom. After all, you wouldn't be around without her.

Keep in mind, though, that no matter how many poems or letters you write her, the most impressive monument that you'll ever erect in her memory is a pure, godly life. I hope this book on Proverbs has supplied you with some of the building materials you'll need. By the way, how is construction going?

11

TREASURE
HUNT

In December 1986 a man in Massachusetts bought a lottery ticket at a local variety store. Without informing his wife of the purchase, he laid the ticket inside a kitchen cabinet. When the drawing for the $5.8 million jackpot occurred, two winning numbers were announced. But only one winner came forward. In an effort to locate the missing winner, officials announced that the other ticket—worth $2.9 million—had been sold at the same variety store where Tom, the man in Massachusetts, had purchased his ticket. Since no one else had claimed the prize, odds were that Tom's ticket had the winning digits.

When he found out where the missing ticket had been purchased, Tom dashed home faster than a track star on steroids. A couple hours earlier, though, the ticket had been escorted to the dump with the rest of the trash! Tom's wife had thrown away the priceless piece of paper without realizing its value.

Neither Tom nor his wife slept well that night. He and a group of friends spent the next two days raking through mounds of trash at the dump in an attempt to find the bag containing his ticket. But they came up empty ("Search For Lottery Ticket Futile," *The Columbia Record,* Columbia, S.C., 17 December 1986).

Though it's against my convictions to purchase a lottery ticket, I feel sorry for Tom. A treasure was his to claim, but he treated the ticket too flippantly. The doorway to riches was only an arm's length away, yet he failed to open it. If only. . . .

Tom's experience reminds me of an unfortunate situation in the spiritual realm. Many Christians treat their ticket to spiritual valuables nonchalantly. There is a wealth of wisdom stored in the vault of God's Word, but we seldom make withdrawals. For instance, a recent poll of Christian teens discovered that only *three percent* of them had a daily devotional time!

I like money as well as the next guy. Yet such neglect of an *eternal* treasure of divine origin is far more tragic than losing a winning lottery ticket.

Why don't people consult the Bible more often? One reason is a lack of know-how. When we try to read the Bible without a simple, structured procedure, its contents may seem as dull as the fiftieth rerun of a chewing gum commercial. Knowing *how* to approach the text increases the likelihood of hitting the jackpot.

Reading Proverbs on your own is better for your spiritual health than digesting what I have to say about it. That's why I want to wrap up this book by equipping you to make your own discoveries. Richard Warren agrees that self-discovery from Scripture is tastier than munching on secondhand insights.

> If I were to meet a starving man by the side of a river, lake, or ocean I could do one of two things: I could get my fishing rod and catch him a fish, thus satisfying his hunger for a few hours; or I could teach him how to fish, thus satisfying his hunger for a lifetime. The second option is obviously the best way to help that man. In the same way, hungry Christians need to be taught how to feed themselves from the Word of God (*12 Dynamic Bible Study Methods*, Victor Books).

As you read this final chapter, open your mental filters to the following perspectives and tips on Bible study.

Hunting Instructions

The following observations can improve your chances of striking it rich in the Book of Proverbs:

1. Realize that God wants to spend time with you! Don't read the Bible to fulfill a religious requirement, or to ease pangs of guilt. Read it because it's a means of deepening your relationship with the Lord. Sure, you need the nourishment of God's Word to strengthen you for daily living. You can't stick to your convictions or make an impact for God without a steady diet of spiritual food. Yet more important than the benefits *you* receive is the impact of your devotional time on your relationship with the Lord. Believe it or not, *He* enjoys one-on-one encounters with *you.*

In a best-selling booklet about the Christian life, *My Heart—Christ's Home* (InterVarsity), Robert

Munger tells how this perspective revolutionized his attitude toward Bible study and prayer. The following excerpt begins with an imaginary conversation between Jesus and Munger. Jesus is speaking in regard to the author's tendency as a young adult to neglect his devotional life:

> "The trouble with you is this: You have been thinking of the quiet time, of the Bible study and prayer time, as a factor in your own spiritual progress, but you have forgotten that this hour means something to me also. Remember, I love you. I have redeemed you at great cost. I desire your fellowship. Now," he said, "do not neglect this hour if only for my sake. Whatever else may be your desire, remember I want your fellowship!"
>
> You know, the truth that Christ wants my fellowship, that He loves me, wants me to be with Him, wants to be with me and waits for me, has done more to transform my quiet time with God than any other single fact.

2. Set realistic goals for your Bible reading. To resolve to spend an hour a day alone with the Lord is a noble objective. But is it achievable? If you've been neglecting prayer and Bible reading, to go from 0 to 60 minutes overnight calls for a major overhaul in your schedule. Think of it this way: if you set a lofty devotional goal of 60 minutes, then you stop after 20, you're a failure — at least when evaluated by the standard you set. You may feel shot down because you fell short of prior expectations. Yet the truth is, 20 minutes a day may represent a big improvement over the past! Setting goals too high merely saps your motivation.

I know someone who started a "9:59" Bible reading club. He committed to 9 minutes and 59 seconds a day. His success at squeezing this small chunk of time from his busy schedule gave him an appetite for more. Before long, he was up to 19:59 a day! Changes are more apt to stick if we take small steps instead of long strides.

3. *Cultivate a willingness to work hard.* Even when your reading takes only a few minutes, hitting the jackpot requires focused attention on the text. To skim a chapter with your eyelids at half-mast, or while bouncing to the beat on your favorite radio station, is a waste of time. You'll need discipline because spine-tingling moments of ecstasy during Bible study are the exceptions, rather than the rule. Take Gary Dausey's words to heart:

Maybe you think you're always going to be blessed and encouraged the second you start to read God's Word. But the plain fact is you must force yourself to sit down and read the Word. Everything else will seem more interesting and more important.

Even after reading for awhile, you may not feel a big emotional closeness to God. But consistency in reading will give you spiritual stamina, as a bowl of hot oatmeal gives you energy on a cold day, even if you don't love every spoonful (from "Come Alive," *Campus Life* magazine).

In the same article, Dausey also emphasizes that the hard work of Bible reading takes the form of observing details of the text.

An old Indian asked a stranger if he had seen

the man who had stolen his guns. The Indian went on to say that the man was young, short, heavy, and spoke with an Eastern accent. The stranger said, "You must must have gotten a good look at him."

"No," was the Indian's reply. "I knew he was young because his footprints in the snow were crisp and showed no signs of dragging feet. He was short because he stood on a box to get to the guns. He was heavy because his footprints sank deep into the snow. He had an Eastern accent because he wore shoes and no cowboy boots."

The Indian knew what to look for—and so can you when it comes to reading God's Word.

The Bible study method you'll encounter later in this chapter will tell you what to look for in Proverbs. It will serve as a map to help you find spiritual treasures. You'll learn to investigate a chapter with the precision of a private eye. As you work at Bible study though, expect to go through at least three stages in your attitude. Howard Hendricks was the speaker who defined the stages for me:

● the "castor oil" stage—when you study the Bible because you know it's good for you, but it isn't too enjoyable.

● the "cereal" stage—when your Bible reading is dry and uninteresting, yet you realize it's nourishing.

● the "peaches and cream" stage—when you begin enjoying the taste of God's Word.

4. Set a definite time of day for your Bible reading. Set your alarm 15 minutes early each morning. Or reserve the last few minutes before bedtime. The time of day isn't necessarily important, but committing to a set time increases the likelihood of consistency.

Some of us are zombies before 9:00 AM, but perky at 11:00 PM. Don't think you get extra credit with God if you read your Bible before breakfast. It all depends on how God put you together. A girl who has her time alone with God at night said, "If the Lord had intended for me to get up with the sunrise, He would have scheduled it later in the day!"

5. *To keep your rendezvous with God fresh, occasionally read a chapter from two or three different translations.* Start with a paraphrase such as *The Living Bible,* then mull over the same chapter from a literal translation such as the *New International Version* (NIV). Prayerfully look at the text through different lenses, and you won't just *own* a *Living Bible* — you'll *be* one! After all, the best Bible translation is when we translate what we read into daily experience.

The "Character" Method

Over the years, I've read Proverbs hundreds of times. Recently I asked the Lord for a simple but systematic way to help others claim its treasure. The result is a nine-step method for exploring each chapter of Proverbs. Each step in the process is actually a *cue* — a signal for you to look for a particular topic, or a specific type of content. This approach is based on the "You're more likely to find something if you're looking for it" principle. It serves the same purpose as a metal detector: the method helps you locate treasure that's buried beneath the surface of the Bible text. I'll explain each step, and illustrate the process from my reading in Proverbs 15.

COMMUNICATION. Start your devotional time by communicating with the Lord. Ask Him to increase your powers of observation, to show you how verses in the chapter relate to your life. Make King David's prayer in Psalm 119:18 your own. "Open my eyes, that I may see wonderful things in Your law."

HOME. No matter how you rate your family life, an important context for applying Bible truths is the home. As you read a chapter, try to link its content to situations around the house. Does a verse make you think of your relationship with Mom or Dad? With a brother or sister? Does it commend or reprove you about your behavior around the house? A sensitive person could make a connection between almost every verse and his homelife. So to keep you from getting bogged down, on any given day just look for *one* verse or insight that's relevant to this area of your life.

As I read Proverbs 15, I pondered this question: *Which verse or truth speaks loudest to things I'm currently experiencing at home?* God's Spirit directed my attention to verse 1. "A gentle answer turns away wrath, but a harsh word stirs up anger." I recalled a recent incident when I reprimanded my two sons for arguing. I corrected them with harsh words of my own. What an example! I yelled at them for yelling at each other! Because I was thinking in terms of a family context, I quickly saw a connection between the verse and my experience. The verse nudged me to confess to the Lord, and to apologize to the boys.

ATTITUDES. An attitude is the feeling or internal reaction we have toward a person or circumstance. Terms like hateful, humble, joyous, teachable, pessimistic, and thankful describe attitudes. As you read each chapter in Proverbs, seek answers to these questions: *What attitudes is the Lord complimenting? What attitudes is He discouraging?* Then bridge the gap from the printed page to your life by pinpointing one attitude to either cultivate or discard.

This cue made me sensitive to Proverbs 15:31. "He who listens to a life-giving rebuke will be at home among the wise." That verse exalts a teachable spirit, a willingness to learn from others' input. The Lord reminded me of how valuable critics are to my ministries of teaching and writing. He doesn't ask me to agree with every critic, but He does expect me to listen. The day I stop learning from others is the day my effectiveness starts to wane.

RELATIONSHIPS. *What connections do you see between chapter content and relationships outside the home?* Friends, teachers, coaches, teammates, and even cold-blooded enemies are potential targets for the transfer of God's Word into your life. Does a verse cause you to evaluate the effect a companion is having on your attitudes or values? Does a line of copy prick your conscience, and remind you to apologize for a comment you made? Does a statement increase your appreciation for a particular friend? The gamut of possibilities seems endless.

When I viewed Proverbs 15 through the lens of "relationships," my eyes stopped at verse 22. "Plans fail for lack of counsel, but with many advisers they succeed." I had been wrestling with a decision for days, but couldn't sort through the issues to my satisfaction. The verse reproved me for my solo effort and prodded me to make an appointment with a close friend. His input clarified my alternatives and removed the static from my brain.

ACTIONS. Numerous one-liners in Proverbs refer to deeds or behavior patterns which God either applauds or denounces. In each chapter, try to pinpoint one behavior that God wants you to either curb or

implement. James urged his readers to "prove yourselves doers of the Word, and not merely hearers"
(James 1:22, NASB).

By now you realize that these nine steps aren't mu-
tually exclusive. One of the other cues might prod you
to *act* differently as well. That's OK. Yet it's possible
that the word "action" will make you aware of a need
that none of the other steps discloses. But heed this
warning: Don't compile a long list of action plans from
each chapter. Trying to obey a lot of things at once will
overload your circuits and cause frustration.

The "Home" phase of the study convicted me
about a harsh tone of voice I had used with my boys.
A few minutes later, as I meditated on the chapter in
light of the "Actions" concept, God's Spirit reminded
me again to apologize to my kids later in the day.
Two different observation cues worked in tandem to
goad me into action.

CONSEQUENCES. It's common for a proverb to
mention either *negative consequences* or *positive results* of a specific attitude or course of action. If you're
looking for such references, you're more likely to
hear God's voice whisper a personal word to you.
What you read may serve as a restraint to some attitudes or behaviors, and an incentive for others.

Here's a verse that warned me about the damaging
consequences of pride: "The Lord tears down the
proud man's house" (15:25). That remark reminded
me of a verse I had memorized from another chapter
in Proverbs. "Pride goes before destruction, and a
haughty spirit before a fall" (16:18). The reference to
pride reminded me to thank the Lord once again for
the success of a recent seminar I had led. When I
accept the credit which *He* deserves, the seed of
pride has a fertile soil in which to grow.

TELLING. Pick one truth or verse from the chapter to pass along to someone else. Did a remark encourage you? Could someone you know receive the same benefit if you shared it? Did God's Spirit expose a problem that you need to share with a friend for the purpose of prayer support? Ask the Lord for an appropriate moment during the day to tell what you learned: over the phone, in a conversation at work, or even in a letter. Remember—the Lord doesn't bless or teach us solely for our own benefit.

The Dead Sea is a lake occupying the southern end of the Jordan River Valley. Its northern tip rests near the city of Jerusalem. This sheet of greenish, salty water is 11 miles across at its widest point, and almost 50 miles long. The water itself is marked by a distinctively bitter taste and a nauseous smell. Do you know why it's called the "Dead" Sea? The water contains so many minerals, such as bromide and sulphur, that few living things can survive in it. The water houses these minerals and can't support many life forms like a normal lake for one basic reason: *the Dead Sea has inlets, but no outlets.* Millions of tons of water—from the Jordan and several smaller streams—flow into the basin daily. But no streams flow out of it to other parts of the country. This salty sea would be fresh or only mildly saline if it had an outlet. The landlocked basin in which it rests in that hot and arid climate serves as a gigantic evaporating pan. Flooding is prevented because the dry heat rapidly evaporates the water.

This fact about the Dead Sea reflects a truth of Christian living: we need to construct outlets so that whatever blessings flow into our lives eventually refresh others as well. Our lives aren't as fresh, reproductive, and attractive if what we're learning and experiencing isn't channeled toward others with whom we have contact.

ENTREATING. "Entreat" is a verb that means to ask or plead. You launched your study time by asking the Lord to show you relevant truths. Now you wrap it up by asking Him to help you carry out the action plan you've identified, cultivate or discard an attitude unveiled by the chapter, or transform a relationship you're concerned about. This prayer acknowledges that fleshing out Bible truth is an unnatural phenomenon requiring *supernatural* aid. Even a spiritual Hercules like the Apostle Paul relied on Christ's power rather than his own: "I can do everything *through Him who gives me strength* (Philippians 4:13, emphasis mine).

REMEMBERING. Which maxim from the chapter impressed you most or left the biggest dent on your conscience? Store that verse in your memory bank. Memorizing a verse gives the Holy Spirit fuel to work with throughout the day, and increases your likelihood of application. King David recognized the practical value of memorizing Scripture. "I have hidden Your Word in my heart that I might not sin against You" (Psalm 119:11).

Since the Lord had used Proverbs 15:1 to convict me of a rude tone of voice around the house, that's the verse I selected to memorize. Now when I'm tempted to overact during a clash, these words automatically surface on the screen of my mind: "A gentle answer turns away wrath, but a harsh word stirs up anger." The memorized verse spurs me to whisper an S.O.S. prayer, and keeps me from a major blowup.

There's an easy way to remember the series of study steps I've explained. The first letters of the key words form an acrostic: C-H-A-R-A-C-T-E-R. Exercise this chapter method throughout Proverbs, and

God will beef up *your* character. What Paul said about the Bible in general rings true of Proverbs in particular. "All Scripture is God-breathed and is useful for teaching, rebuking, correcting and training in righteousness" (2 Timothy 3:16).

Remember Tom, the fellow whose winning lottery ticket wound up at the town dump? How are *you* treating *your* ticket to God's bounty? Try this CHARACTER method for a month, and you'll find treasure instead of trash.

A NOTE FROM THE AUTHOR

Letters are a "first-class" way to communicate. If I've said anything in this book that you'd like to salute, shoot down, or discuss at greater length, drop me a note. Or if you want to write for some other reason, your letter would still be the highlight of my day. My address is:

Terry Powell
Columbia Bible College
P.O. Box 3122
Columbia, SC 29230

P.S. I'll answer your letter.